AMERICAN FURNITURE OF THE 19TH CENTURY 1840-1880

Revised & Expanded 2nd Edition

Eileen and Richard Dubrow

4880 Lower Valley Road, Atglen, PA 19310 USA

This book is dedicated to our children: Gail, David, Karen and Marc for their patience and help with this book and for their forbearance for the time it took away from them.

The prices herein were provided by Brad and Brian Witherell. Brad and Brian Witherell of Witherell's in Elk Grove, California are certified and nationally recognized appraisers. They are regular participants on Public Television's *Antiques Roadshow* and work with some of the nation's leading museums and collectors as both appraisers and dealers. Additionally, they have lectured on the subject of antiques and authored two books for Schiffer Publishing Ltd., *California's Best; Old West Art and Antiques* and *Late 19th Century Furniture by Berkey and Gay.* Together they operate a private gallery that specializes in investment quality mid-19th century American furniture, antique firearms, edged weapons, and art and antiques of the American West. They can be reached at www.witherells.com or by telephone at 916-683-3266.

These estimated prices are based on the objects being in original condition. Also, furniture attributed to or believed to be the work of J.H. Belter & Company is assumed to be in rosewood unless otherwise noted.

Revised price guide:2000

Library of Congress Card Number: 00-100615

Typeset in Aldine 721 BT

ISBN: 0-7643-1080-1
Printed in China
1 2 3 4

Published by Schiffer Publishing Ltd.
4880 Lower Valley Road
Atglen, PA 19310
Phone: (610) 593-1777; Fax: (610) 593-2002
E-mail: Schifferbk@aol.com
Please visit our web site catalog at **www.schifferbooks.com**

In Europe, Schiffer books are distributed by Bushwood Books
6 Marksbury Avenue Kew Gardens
Surrey TW9 4JF England
Phone: 44 (0)208-392-8585; Fax: 44 (0)208-392-9876
E-mail: Bushwd@aol.com
Free postage in the UK., Europe; air mail at cost.

This book may be purchased from the publisher.
Include $3.95 for shipping. Please try your bookstore first.
We are always looking for authors to write books on new and related subjects.
If you have an idea for a book please contact us at the address above.
You may write for a free printed catalog.

Acknowledgments

Each new book owes a debt to the books, people and institutions that precede and inspire it. We are grateful to them and the following people and staffs for their time and the courtesies they extended to us. We hope we have included everyone; any omission is merely an oversight.

We acknowledge our thanks to: Mr. and Mrs. Jay Anderson; Lee B. Anderson; W.T. Barnes and Company; John L. Blocker; David Bolten; Boston Museum of Fine Arts; The Brooklyn Museum; Dr. and Mrs. Milton Brinley; Morris Butler House; Margaret Cauldwell; Chicago Historical Society; William Doyle; Joy Freeman; Grand Rapids Public Library; Dr. and Mrs. John Heavron; Mr. and Mrs. Donald Hurst; Mr. and Mrs. Richard Hurst; Indianapolis Museum of Art; Mr. and Mrs. Ed Kennedy; Lyndhurst, Tarrytown, New York; Mr. and Mrs. R. Manney; Lockwood Mathews Mansion; Richard McGeehan; Mr. and Mrs. James Mello; Metropolitan Museum of Art; Munson-Williams-Proctor Institute; Museum of the City of New York; Museum of Fine Arts, Houston; Milo M. Naeve, Art Institute of Chicago; Newark Museum; New York Historical Society; Grant Oakes; Philadelphia Museum of Art; Ramsey Pope Hause; Richardson Bates House; Rodris Roth; Dr. and Mrs. Sanders; Marvin Schwartz; Robert Skinner; The Smithsonian Institution; Edward J. Stanek; Dr. and Mrs. J. Steichen; E. and C. Stone; Sunnyside, Irvington-on-Hudson; Douglas K. True; Coley Volpiani; Betty Lawson Walters; William Watkins; and Yale University.

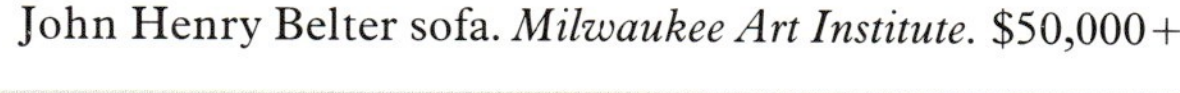
John Henry Belter sofa. *Milwaukee Art Institute.* $50,000+

Preface

"Furniture, whether useful or merely ornamental, at once reveals its own story of the degree of talent and the length of time devoted to its execution."

Cabinetmakers and the furniture of the mid-nineteenth century is a field in its infancy. While a great deal is known about the various styles and their popularity and about some of the makers of these styles, there is not a vast amount that can be documented as made by a particular cabinet shop.

We are attempting in this book to put together the bits and pieces that are known. To show wherever possible documented and/or labeled pieces or strongly attributed ones. We would be the first ones to recognize that our task is far from complete. We intend to go on learning and welcome all documented information on either cabinetmakers or their furniture. There were thousands of cabinetmakers across the United States and many thousands of pieces of furniture. Most of these pieces are unidentified today. We hope to encourage the identification of those pieces and the cabinetmakers.

We have attempted to put the styles in chronological order where possible. Several of the cabinetmakers, however, worked over long periods and in a variety of styles. The most prominent examples are the firms of J. and J. W. Meeks who made Gothic, Rococo and Empire Rococo styles. The fancifullness of George Hunzinger's work makes classification difficult, and this is even truer of the Herter Brothers furniture.

Therefore, we have included what we know about some of the most prominent makers and rely on our readers to help us find new information to pursue so that we all can obtain a clearer picture of "American Furniture of the Nineteenth Century."

Richard and Eileen Dubrow
January 1983

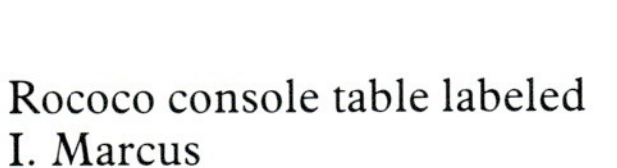

Rococo console table labeled I. Marcus

Opposite:
Labeled couch by John H. Belter that documents unlaminated work by Mr. Belter. Probably made to match a bedroom suite. *Collection of R. & E. Dubrow.*

Contents

Historical Background

When we collect antiques, sooner or later we must realize that we are really collecting social history in concrete form. Social history is a reflection of the national events which determine whether a country is a user or supplier of raw materials. Social history reflects economic shifts between countries which effect personal wealth and taste. One indication of social taste is household furnishings.

In the late eighteenth century, French society was considered "in good taste" by world standards, and furniture in the French social structure was defeated and replaced.

As the American society became increasingly a supplier of raw materials (food and cotton) and manufactured goods, the people were able to afford and strained to develop their own culture. In relation to domestic furnishings, America wanted its own style. The creation of that style is the real subject of this book; what the "rags-to-riches" society created.

To set the stage on a world scale, we shall briefly review events of world history which affected and inspired American cabinetmakers to create the American styles. Since nineteenth-century America was an amalgamation of foreign people, the culture they created was also mixed, and the furniture styles which evolved were vastly dissimilar. Together, however, they reflect American taste in the home.

In the sixteenth and seventeenth centuries, Europe was pushing out its geographical boundaries by colonizing. Settlers were sent to new lands from Spain, England and France. The Spanish settled up through Central America and as far north as Florida. The French settled what is today Canada, and traveled down the Great Lakes, following the Mississippi River to its mouth at New Orleans. The English came here last and settled the coastal strip from Maine almost to Florida.

Since the settlers in America had abundant land, plentiful labor and scarce capital, they turned to agriculture. Each region of this new land has different product potential, but each had the incentive to produce items for markets outside the immediate area, so that needed items could be imported.

The Southern region produced rice, tobacco, indigo, and later the cotton that England needed. The middle Colonies (New York, New Jersey, and Pennsylvania) had fertile land on which grain and livestock could be efficiently raised. Since these were products that the English also produced, the middle colonies traded more with southern Europe and the West Indies. In New England, an increasing percentage of people turned to the sea to earn their living. They not only became a major shipping power for the other colonies, but for England as well.

Thriving agriculture and vigorous export trade made Americans wealthy and able to buy more goods from England and the Continent to raise their standard of living. After the revolution, America's economy emerged from colonial status to a period of turmoil with confederation, and then on to enjoy an era of prosperity and economic growth.

John Henry Belter rosewood, pierced carved, laminated child's chair. *Richard and Eileen Dubrow.* $5000-7000

The struggle between the French and the English in the New World was inevitable. There had been conflict for generations in Europe, and the relations were no better in the New World where their empires lay side by side. The wars began in 1690 with the massacre by French and Indian raiders of English settlers at Schenectady, New York and ended with the capture by the English of Quebec in 1759 and Montreal in 1760. This last struggle was the most important and proved to be the beginning of the end of French power in North America. When the diplomats gathered in Paris in February of 1763 to make peace, France gave up an empire by signing Canada over to England and by giving up any claims to territory between the Alleghenies and the Mississippi River. For helping the Bourbons, Spain had to give up Florida and any rights she had east of the Mississippi in order to regain Cuba. With this territorial gain, England emerged as the most powerful nation in the world.

Until the mid-eighteenth century, England made no effort to control the expansion of her American colonies. Colonial affairs were often neglected or badly mismanaged. Under King George III, (1760-1820) the British decided that the American colonies ought to pay the debts that had been incurred by the French and Indian wars. New taxes were introduced. Colonial leaders decided that, since they were not represented in Parliament, the taxes were unconstitutional. George III refused to change his stand. War broke out between the colonists and England. France sided with the colonists. Britain was defeated, and George III continued his struggle for power until his mind broke and he went mad. George III, therefore, became best known as the King who lost the thirteen colonies.

George III was followed by George IV from 1820-1830. William IV reigned from 1830-37, and England itself was on the verge of revolution. The Whigs were able to break the power of the Tories, and gave power to the middle class by providing seats in The House of Commons for the representatives of factory towns. In 1837, Victoria, granddaughter of George III, mounted the throne. She reigned until her death in 1901.

Victoria was eighteen years old when she was crowned on June 28, 1838. During her reign, customs duties on imported grain were lifted, working men were given the right to vote, the country developed a network of railways and highways, the population increased threefold, and the middle class became prosperous. The working class was more comfortable than it had ever been before. England also fought the Boer War between 1899-1902 and the Crimean War between 1854-56.

During the years Victoria reigned, the United States had eighteen presidents and became a world power.

The presidents were:

Martin Van Buren	1837-41
William Henry Harrison	1841
John Tyler	1841-45
James Knox Polk	1845-49
Zachary Taylor	1849-50
Millard Fillmore	1850-54
Franklin Pierce	1854-57
James Buchanan	1857-61
Abraham Lincoln	1861-65
Andrew Johnson	1865-69
Ulysses S. Grant	1869-77
Rutherford Hayes	1877-81
James A. Garfield	1881
Chester A. Arthur	1881-85
Grover Cleveland	1885-89
Benjamin Harrison	1889-93
Grover Cleveland	1893-97
William McKinley	1897-1901

Parlor furniture in "Afton Villa near St. Francisville, Louisiana, possibly by Siebricht. This furniture was later used in "Melrose" after reupholstery by Siebrecht. *Photograph courtesy of William Barrow Floyd.* $8000-12,000 (3 pcs.)

Ladies' writing desk which converts to a card table by Elija Galusha. *Photograph courtesy of the Rensselaer County of New York Historical Society.* $2000-3000

Extra-Grade Wooton Cylinder desk shown open and closed. $8000-12,000

Many of these United States presidents directed the expansion of the country and influenced its economic growth. While England had a single Victorian era, this country had a series of periods when American ingenuity made America a world power.

The history of France from the seventeenth through the nineteenth centuries differs markedly from that of the Untied States. Louis XIV (1643-1715) took the sun as his symbol, he was a pleasure seeker. He financed the arts and sciences and through his minister, Colbert, promoted commerce and industry. His great-grandson Louis XV was crowned King at age 5 in 1714 and ruled with a regent, Duke Philip II of Orleans, until he became 18.

Louis XV reigned until 1774. His court was the inheritor of luxury initiated by Louis XIV and excellent business practices established by Colbert. In this age the high style Baroque was born with its swirls, curls, feathers, frills, rocks, shells, gold leaf, and ormolu. By 1770 there was as much sentiment for revolution among the downtrodden in France as there was among the American colonists.

When Louis XVI came to the throne in 1774, his queen, Marie Antoninette of Austria, wanted to continue the gay pleasures of her predecessors. France, however was sympathetic to the American revolutionaries against George III of England. After their own revolution in 1789, a period of turmoil was followed by the Directory which came into power in 1795. Worse crimes were committed in the name of liberty than any King had ever dreamed. Out of this turmoil came the "Directoire" style of French furniture developed by Louis David for Louis XVI's court. In America later, Duncan Phyfe of New York, and Henry Connelly of Philadelphia embraced this style.

When Napoleon Bonaparte ruled France in 1804, his ambition, energy and ability put France back as a world power. At this time a new furniture style developed called "Empire". When Napoleon was exiled to Elba in 1814, Louis XVIII (grandson of Louis XV) became King, but in 1815 Napoleon escaped from Elba, and within three weeks he was again Emperor. This second Empire lasted one hundred days. Napoleon was exiled this time to St. Helena and Louis XVIII reigned again until 1824.

King Charles X succeeded Louis XVIII and reigned until 1830. He named his grandson as his successor with Louis Philippe as Regent. The Chamber of Deputies, however, named Louis Philippe as King. In his reign the furniture style of Louis XV was revived. During this period a "Second Baroque" style took France by storm, crossed the Atlantic as "The French Antique Style" and captured the heart of the United States.

By 1831, United States craftsmen were making furniture in the Empire style and fancy grained chairs of the Directoire, (yet the old favorite Chippendale was still retained). Mansions were being built in the United States along the Hudson, Delaware, James, Savannah and Ohio Rivers. Into these mansions went French rugs, French wallpaper, French furniture, French draperies, lamps and clocks. This "Second Baroque" revival came to the United States at a time when craftsmen had discovered mass production. This was the secret whereby a luxury of any kind could be converted into a staple. While the French had revived the "Second Baroque" style to change the state of mind of its people, the United States accepted it because we had discovered mass production to be the secret of common wealth creation.

The years 1815-60 were the period of America's greatest growth acceleration. As the separate regions in the United States became more specialized, each concentrated on producing commodities and exchanging them with the other regions. The South traded cotton with England, which at this time was in the midst of an industrial revolution, and imported foodstuffs, and manufactured goods, crude and fine. The South also depended on the West for corn, wheat and livestock supplied by steamboats after invention in 1811. By 1817, seventeen steamboats were on the American rivers and by 1855 there were seven hundred twenty seven. The Northeast also discovered larger Southern and Western markets for manufactured goods in exchange for food. This was the economic pivot upon which the American economy swung during the period 1815-60.

Inventions and technology were the order of the day. Eli Whitney's invention of the cotton gin enabled the South to concentrate on cotton. In 1814, the power loom invented by Francis Cabot meant spinning and carding in a single plant. Elias Howe's sewing machine in 1846 revived the northeast plants. By 1830 the circular saw was in use. By 1840 Thomas Blanchard had introduced the band saw. The mining of nickel, copper, lead and zinc was well established by 1830. Coal gas was produced for use in lighting for most urban centers by 1825. During this period glass manufactories and iron foundries were established in most sizable towns, allowing us to manufacture more lamps between 1830 and 1870 than in all the preceding decades. By 1859, when petroleum was pumped from drilled wells, everyone was in line for better lighting. William Kelley's discovery of the Bessemer process in 1851 made another leap forward in industrialization possible. By 1860 trains were running regularly between Baltimore, Philadelphia, New York and Boston. These cities were linked by rail to Cleveland, Cincinnati, Chicago and St. Louis. The major cities of the South were joined by railroads and then connected to the Northern network of rail lines. This allowed travel time to be cut from weeks to days and the cost of carrying freight to be cut from dollars to cents per ton-mile.

Before 1850 the chief economic class had been merchants who handled imports, exports and interstate commerce. After 1850, the role of the manufacturer was magnified. As opportunities for manufacturing multiplied, individual enterprises found their own resources inadequate and banded together in corporations to raise larger capital. These concerns sold stock to the public and borrowed from the banks. A new class of businessmen emerged, including the manufacturer, inventor, industrial banker, corporate lawyer and industrial manager. This growing upper middle class was firmly in power by the latter half of the nineteenth century, but in general they were not secure or creative. As a group, they preferred to reinterpret established forms of furniture in their homes to display "solid quality" to their peers. They required ready-made backgrounds that were showy, respectable, durable but not too modern. The waves of immigrants particularly the German carvers in the 1840's, were able to interpret a variety of furniture styles for these people.

"Extra-Grade" Wooton Patent Secretary as it was exhibited at the Indiana State Museum. $25,000-35,000

Whereas in colonial time furniture in the United States had English prototypes, (Chippendale 1755-90; Sheraton and Hepplewhite 1790-1810) and French styles prevailed from 1800 to 1835, from 1835 onward America emerged with its own furniture and architecture. As a world power and economic leader, America created during the nineteenth century a true American furniture style based on its own needs, designs, and wants.

It is for this reason that we ought now to drop the term "Victorian" for American nineteenth century furniture from our vocabulary. We should replace this term with the names of the styles evident in the United States between 1830-76:

Gothic	1830-1840
Rococo	1840-1860
Elizabethan	1850-1870
Renaissance	1860-1875
Aesthetic Movement Fore-runners	1865-1890
Louis XVI-revival	1860-1880
Neo Grec	1870-1880
Moorish	1876-1900

It is from this point of view that the following chapters are organized.

Cabinetmakers

Allen and Brothers
Philadelphia, Pennsylvania
Business address: 1847 - 119 Spruce Street
1850 - 137 Walnut Street and factory at 12th & Pleasant Streets
Furniture style: Rococo

William Allen Sr., established a business in 1835 dealing in rare and fancy woods as well as furniture. His sons William Jr., and Joseph succeeded him in business and were listed in the Philadelphia directory of 1847. Their factory remained at 12th and Pleasant Streets between 1850 and the late 1860's. By 1869 William, Junior, is no longer listed, and Joseph was a partner with another brother, James C. Allen, who was in charge of their wareroom and upholstery shop. In 1902 James C. Allen closed the business. Allen and Brothers carried only fine goods and was known for custom cabinet work.

Annesby and Vint
Albany, New York
Business Address:
1885 - Annesby and Company, 57 North Pearl Street and 506 Broadway

Annesby and Vint were cabinetmakers in Albany between 1866 and 1885. As Annesby and Company the firm continued until 1945.

J.S.L. Babbs
Boston, Massachusetts
Business Address:
6 1/2 Albany Block, Albany Street
Furniture style: Rococo

J.S.L. Babbs made "antique furniture", assumed to mean he worked in the style of Louis XV with swirls, curls and gilding.

John Henry Belter
New York, New York
Business address:
1844 - 40 1/2 Chatham Street
1846-1852 - 372 Broadway
1853 - 547 Broadway

Opposite Page
Oil painting of room interior of the 1840 period. *Photograph courtesy of Frank S. Schwartz & Son.*

1856 -552 Broadway
1861 - 722 Broadway
Born: In 1804 in Hitler, Iburg, Hannover, Germany
Died: October 15, 1863 in New York City.
Furniture style: Rococo

Branded John Henry Belter, rosewood dresser. *Richard and Eileen Dubrow.* $30,000-40,000

John Henry Belter left Germany under exit visa #817 from the port of Bremen on September 5, 1833 bound for New York. His passport describes him as 29 years old, five feet, seven inches tall, born and raised in Hilter, jurisdiction of Iburg, Kingdom of Hannover. He had brown hair and eyes, a medium figure, pointed nose, short chin and incomplete teeth. His coloring was described as healthy, and no special marks or scars were listed. He traveled to New York via Bremen although his original plan had been to travel to Baltimore via Drepholy. He traveled alone. On April 11, 1839 John Henry Belter became an American citizen in the Marine Court of the City of New York in Manhattan.

Little is known of his early years in New York from 1833 until 1844 when he opened his first shop at 40 1/2 Chatham Street. But there can be little doubt he worked as a cabinet maker in New York shops. In 1846 he moved to 372 Broadway and stayed there until 1852. In 1853 he moved to 547 Broadway. While retaining this address in April of 1850 he had the architect Louis Berger design a factory for him. It was to be erected on the north side of 76th Street near 3rd Avenue. The front was to be on 76th Street. The building was to be five stories high, with a basement, subcellar and vaults. The front and rear were to be 100 feet wide, while the depth of the building was to be 102 feet two inches. The center core of the building (50 x 50 feet) to be covered with a dome and form an open space. The dome was to be a sixteen sided polygon with thick fluted glass sides. A cupola was to crown the dome, and the surrounding roof was to be tin. The roof was to extend down from the dome to the four corners of the building. All material was to be of the best and all labor the finest.

At about this time his brother-in-law, Jonathan H. Springmeyer joined the firm. In 1856 the firm address is 552 Broadway and in 1861 it is 722 Broadway and two other Springmeyer brothers, William and Frederick had joined the firm.

John H. Belter was married to Louisa Springmeyer. Her family was from the same town as his, Hilter. They had five children.

John Henry (died January 6, 1906)
Augusta (married Joseph Taylor)
Louise
Caroline (Josephine)
Ferdinand

Enlargement of brand on the above dresser.

Detail of top drawer insert of the branded J.H.Belter dresser. *Richard and Eileen Dubrow.*

817 of the Register
Passport For Travel To Foreign Countries
Valid: One Year
DESCRIPTION of Bearer
: 29 years
ght: 5'7"
ıre: Medium
r: Brown
w: Rounded
brows: Brown
e: Pointed
ıth: Medium
h: Incomplete
n: Short
e: Oval
or of Face: Healthy
Special Marks None
Speaks German
Signature of Traveler
BELTER
ł: 10 Groschen

2080

GROSCHEN CONV. MÜNZE

№ 817 des Registers.
Reisepaß für das [illegible] Land.
Gültig für [illegible]

Beschreibung des Inhabers
Alter 29 Jahr
Größe 5 Fuß 7 Zoll Calenb.
Statur [illegible]
Haare [illegible]
Stirn [illegible]
Augenbraunen [illegible]
Augen [illegible]
Nase [illegible]
Mund [illegible]
Zähne [illegible]
Kinn [illegible]
Bart [illegible]
Gesicht [illegible]
Gesichtsfarbe [illegible]
Besondere Zeichen [illegible]
Spricht [illegible]
Unterschrift des Reisenden
[illegible]
Bezahlt 10 [illegible]

Königreich Hannover.

Alle Civil- und Militair-Behörden werden geziemend ersucht, d.. Vorzeiger dieses Johann Heinrich Belter [illegible] bürtig aus / wohnhaft in Hilter Amts Iburg mit [illegible] auf [illegible] behuf [illegible] vorhabenden Reise von hier über Diepholz, Bremen nach Baltimore frei und ungehindert reisen und zurückreisen, ihm auch nöthigen Falls jeden möglichen Schutz angedeihen zu lassen.

Osnabrück, den [illegible] August
Eintausend Achthundert [illegible]

Königliche Polizei-Direction.
p.a. Wieman[illegible]

KINGDOM OF HANNOVER
All Civil and Military Officials are respectfully requested to permit the bearer of this document, Johann Heinrich BELTER, legitimized through a document of his local jurisdiction
born in
residing at HILTER, jurisdiction of IBURG
without companion
to travel freely and without hindrance to investigate methods for his contemplated voyage from here via Diepholz, Bremen to Baltimore back and forth, and, if the necessity arises to give him all feasible protection. OSNABRUECK, the Twentyninth August
One Thousand Eight Hundred Thirty-Three
Official Seal Royal Police Directorate
City of Osnabrueck p.p. Weiman

It is probable that the entire ingmeyer family emigrated to United States since it is own that Mrs. Belter's mother d in this country in 1865 and uried in the same cemetery as n H. Belter and other family mbers. John H. Belter died tober 15, 1863 of a form of tuculosis. He is buried in New k Bay Cemetery in Jersey City, w Jersey. (Lot 752, section K, rth) Some time after Mr. ter's death his wife Louisa rried Belter's former factory nager August Hentz. The firm tinued under his name until 5 and then became ingmeyer Brothers. It was sed finally in 1867 (December when assignment was made by Springmeyers to Thomas rson. Pearson sold the lease

Reverse of passport on previous page.

7 Hbq

Inspected and valid for voyage of
NEW YORK
Bremen, the 5th Sept. 1833

The Police-Directorate
per procura
Wildens

Official Seal

STATE OF NEW-YORK,
CITY AND COUNTY OF NEW-YORK, } ss.

Be it Remembered,

That on the Eleventh day of April in the year of our Lord one thousand eight hundred and thirty Nine

Jn. Belter

at present of the City of New-York. appeared in the MARINE COURT OF THE CITY OF NEW-YORK, (the said Court being a Court of Record, having a common law jurisdiction, and a Clerk and Seal,) and applied to the said Court to be admitted to become a Citizen of the United States of America, pursuant to the directions of the Act of Congress of the United States of America, entitled "An Act to establish an uniform Rule of Naturalization, and to repeal the Acts heretofore passed on that subject; and also to an Act entitled an Act in addition to an Act entitled an Act to establish an uniform Rule of Naturalization, and to repeal the Acts heretofore passed on that subject, and also to an Act entitled "An Act supplementary to the Acts heretofore passed on the subject of an uniform Rule of Naturalization, passed 30th day of July 1813," and to the Act relative to Evidence in cases of Naturalization, passed 22d March, 1816, and an Act, in further addition to an Act, to establish an uniform Rule of Naturalization, and to repeal the acts heretofore passed on that subject, passed May 26th, 1824;" and an Act entitled "An Act to amend the Act concerning Naturalization, passed May 24th, 1828;" And the said Jn. Belter having thereupon produced to the Court such evidence, made such declaration and renunciation, and taken such oaths as are by the said act required:

THEREUPON it was ordered by the said Court, that the said John Belter be admitted, and he was accordingly admitted by the Court, a CITIZEN OF THE UNITED STATES OF AMERICA.

IN TESTIMONY WHEREOF, the Seal of the said Court, is hereunto affixed, this Eleventh day of April in the year [illegible] of the Independence of the United States.

John Marbois[?]

PER CURIAM, CLERK.

J.H. Belter's naturalization paper. He became a citizen on April 11, 1839. Until this paper appeared it was though that he came to New York around 1843.

assigned to him at auction. The Belter estate had to buy this lease in order to own the factory free and clear. The executors also purchased all the Springmeyer machinery at this auction.

The executors then sold the factory and machinery to Blephen, Bolrath and Company for $20,500 plus a house on Lexington Avenue. This house was then sold for $28,000 less its $14,000 mortgage. He did not die a pauper as formerly believed. While has estate was valued at $8,321.00 with additions of $53,022.49 and debts of $37,150.39, by the final accounting of 1865 there was $24,193.90 plus property.

This is what we know of the man - what of his work. John Henry Belter did not invent the process of laminating. Laminating was probably known in Egyptian times. It was used by Robert Adams for chairs in 1773. In the 1820s, Biedemier used bent and veneered woods. What Mr. Belter did do was bring laminated construction to the height of style in the United States. He also bought new methods of molding and bending wood to the cabinet making trade.

On July 31, 1847 (#5208) Mr. Belter patented "Machinery for sawing Arabesque Chairs". This machine formed the basic pattern openings for his pierced carved pieces. It was a variety of jigsaw that allowed the back of the piece to be fixed in position, pierced, and then sawed in any direction. It should be noted that if this saw was patented in 1847, pierced patterns must have been in his first shop from the beginning and not later as once thought.

On August 19, 1856 (#15,552) he patented a laminated bed, in two pieces, held together by a notched internal frame. The staves construction of the bed differed from those on chairs. In this patent, one mold turned out the head and one the foot board. Upholstered tops for the very short side pieces were an optional feature. There is a notation on the patent that the bed could also be made in four pieces. On the four piece bed, two separate side pieces are attached to the head and foot board by interlocking end pieces. The single piece internal frame of the two piece bed is replaced by slats in the four piece bed.

On February 23, 1858 (#19,405) Mr. Belter patented an "Improvement in the method of manufacturing furniture". In this, the rail and stile chair back construction was replaced with a one piece molded back of laminated wood. This made the back not only strong, but beautiful from all sides. In terms of inventiveness, this patent chair back was bent along several planes rather than a single plane. It also showed a method for laminating and molding wood for a number of chair backs at the same time. From the illustration and descriptions in the patent it can be seen that the seams of some of the staves are bound to fall in such a way that there would be hairline seams on chair backs. These hairlines would not always be in the center, and smaller chairs might not have a seam while larger chairs might have two. Six layers are shown in this patent illustration.

Belter's last patent was on January 24, 1860 (#26881) for a bureau drawer. The sides of the drawer are single strips of laminated wood, joined together with a glued scarf and molded in the cawls of proper shape. The drawer bottom is of laminated wood. The molded sides are glued to it in such a way that two of the bottom edges are left projecting. These projecting edges are fitted into grooves cut into the sides of the bureau. This eliminated the need for dust boards between the various drawers. The patent also included a system of locking the various drawers from one drawer.

Contrary to critics of 19th century furniture, regarding the interest of cabinet makers only in piling decoration upon decoration, Mr. Belter's patents show a concern for achieving the simple, lightweight, delicate structures that were necessary to carry out his exuberant decorative designs. He also shows great concern for improved cleanliness and ease in dismantling in case of fire. Not until the Art Nouveau period was Belter equaled in his ability to add carved, scrolled decoration to flowing structures. His chair backs actually had a free form and curve that anticipated the 20th century designs of Charles Eames.

What differentiates Mr. Belter's furniture from other Rococo cabinet makers?

1. Not all his furniture was laminated but on laminated pieces the edges are tapered not cut straight across.
2. Chair backs are attached to seats so that the outer layer of laminate blends with or feathers into and becomes a part of the apron of the chair.
3. Arms and legs of sofas and chairs are carved from single pieces.
4. Sofas and recamere's are upholstered backs, not wood as the chairs are.
5. Some pieces do have applied cresting. (Extra pieces of carving glued to the concave side).
6. On tables, the alternate high and low relief makes the carving appear to be from a solid piece rather than applied to laminated wood.
7. Depending upon the size of the piece seams do appear on the backs of pieces. They are hairline seams.
8. Belter furniture in general is not labeled. A few pieces do exist with paper labels. Pieces covered by patents had impressed brands.
9. All patterns were made throughout his twenty year work span. They were not sequential.
10. Original material found on chairs indicate that original upholstery was silk damask, brocatelle, plain silk and velvet.

John Henry Belter's original patent model chair and details. This model chair shows the "dishing" or "bending" on two planes covered by the 1858 patent. Chair measures 11 13/16" high, 6 1/4" wide, 7 3/4" deep. $50,000+

The first labeled Belter couch, that is not laminated, see page 121, bears the address 522 Broadway. This dates the couch about 1852 when Belter worked at that address. The couch is constructed of 1 1/2 inch solid lengths of rosewood glued together. When the desired height for the back of the couch was achieved a bandsaw was used to cut the shape of the frame. The front and back aprons were also cut on a bandsaw from continuous curves glued together. Feet were cut separately and doweled and glued to the apron. The entire piece was then veneered. Tables are also known to have been made by this method.

Belter table, not laminated. Same construction as couch.
$10,000-15,000

Label affixed to frame of couch.

Construction view.

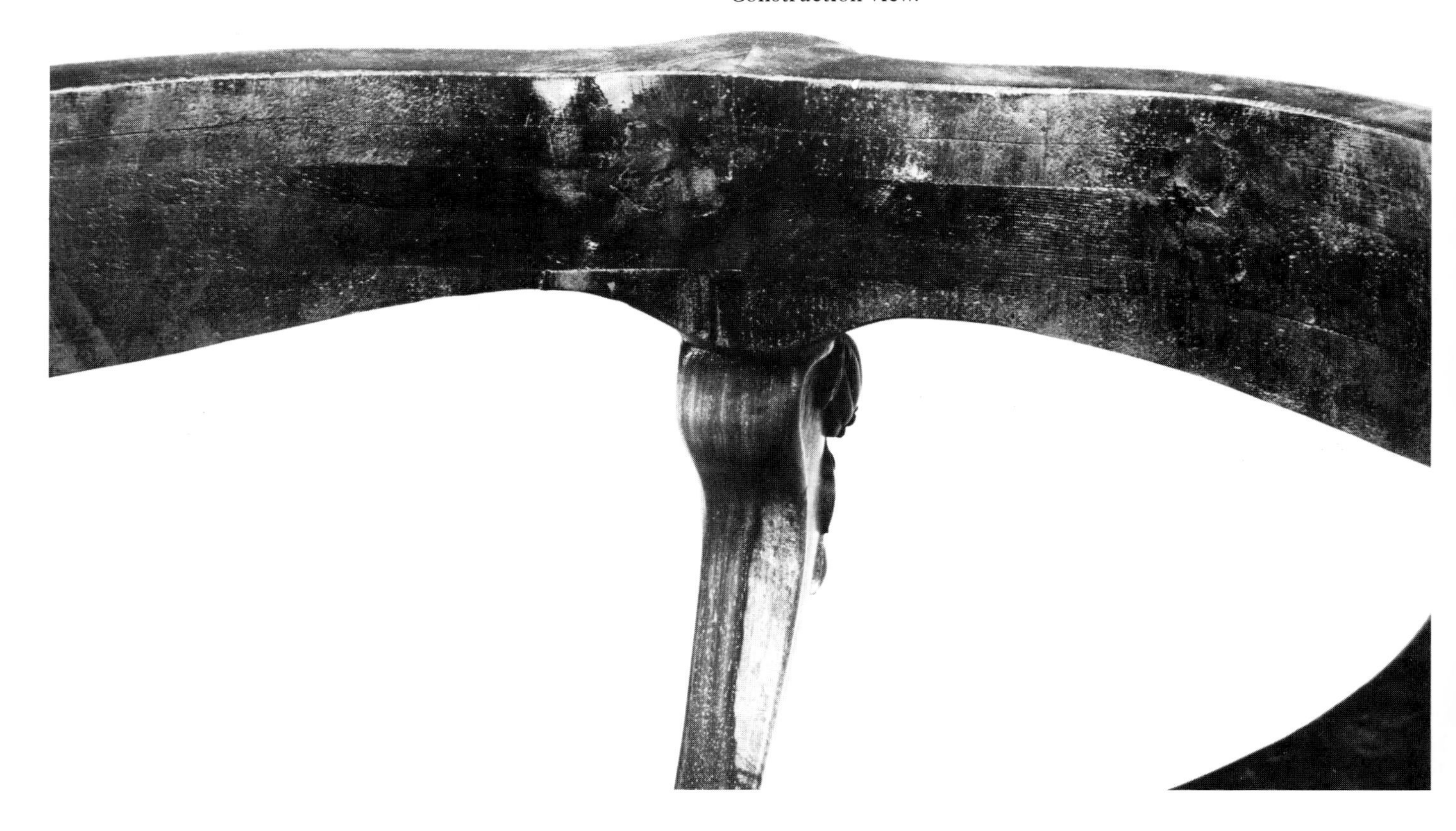

Eli F. Benjamin
Cooperstown, New York
Utica, New York

Eli Benjamin was a cabinetmaker in Cooperstown, New York from 1810 to 1822 when he moved to Utica to form a partnership with William Tillman. When he left, his brother Mills took over the Cooperstown shop. Eli's partnership with Tillman lasted until 1833 when Tillman moved to Geneva, New York. Benjamin and Tillman together made fine quality mahogany chairs. (See also William Tillman)

Julius Berkey
Grand Rapids, Michigan
Business address:
- 1861 - Juluis Berkey
- 1862 - Berkey & Matter
- 1863 - Berkey Brothers & Company
- 1866 - Berkey Brothers & Gay
- 1870 - Berkey & Gay

Furniture style: Renaissance

In 1859, Julius Berkey was making furniture with James Eggleston; and later he went into business with Alphonso Hamm, but neither partnership lasted.

In 1861, Berkey alone opened a furniture shop on the second floor of his brother William's (see also William Berkey) planing mill and sash and door works. In 1862, Julius Berkey and Elias Matter formed a partnership called Berkey & Matter. William bought a half interest in the firm in 1863 and the name became Berkey Brothers and Company and together they manufactured furniture, doors and blinds. George W. Gay bought half of William's interest in 1866 and the name changed to Berkey Brothers and Gay.

Julius's business is best known as Berkey and Gay which was prosperous, for in 1880 the firm employed an average of 400 people. In 1886, David Kendall was their furniture designer, and in March of 1888, W.T. Wilson was the foreman of their factory. Julius Berkey and William R. Fox secured a patent in 1888 for furniture casters.

When George W. Gay died, his son Will H. Gay became head of the company which retained the name Berkey and Gay. Acquisitions enlarged the company in stages as it bought the Oriel Cabinet Company in 1911, and the Wallace Furniture Company and Grand Rapids Upholstering Company in 1926. Then, in 1929, Berkey and Gay was sold to the Simmons Company of Chicago. A year later the firm discontinued production.

In 1935 there was an attempt to reopen the firm, and during the second World War it converted to war work, but post-war attempts to reorganize it were abandoned.

William A. Berkey
Grand Rapids, Michigan
Business address:
- 1863 - Berkey Brothers and Company
- 1866 - Berkey Brothers and Gay
- 1868 - Berkey & Gay
- 1870 - Phoenix Manufacturing Company, Ottawa and Fairbanks Streets

(No Model.)

J. BERKEY & W. R. FOX.

FURNITURE CASTER.

No. 378,649. Patented Feb. 28, 1888.

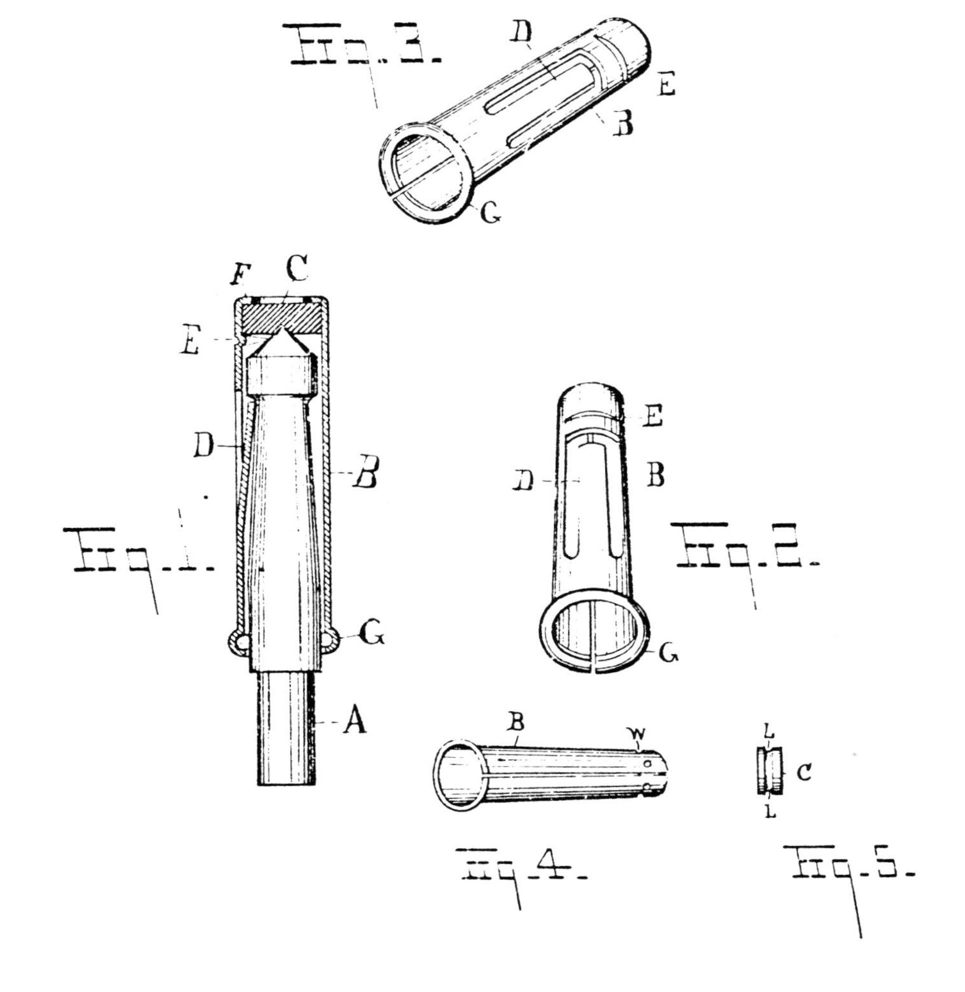

Julius Berkey.
Wm R. Fox,
INVENTORS.

WITNESSES:
Arthur C. Denison.
Allison H. Norden.

BY
Edward Taggart
their ATTORNEY.

1873 - Phoenix Furniture Company, West Fulton and Summer Streets
1882 - William A. Berkey Furniture Company
Furniture style: Renaissance

Before 1861, William A. Berkey ran a planing mill and sash and door works in Grand Rapids, Michigan.

In 1868, William Berkey was a partner in his brother Julius' firm (see also Julius Berkey) Berkey & Gay and was named the assignee for Atkins and Soule, cabinetmakers in Grand Rapids. In 1870, he, Nelson Northrop and Frank McWhoter organized that company into the Phoenix Manufacturing Company which conducted a small furniture making business at the corner of Ottawa and Fairbanks Streets in Grand Rapids.

He withdrew entirely from Berkey and Gay in 1873 to devote his time to building up the company which was reorganized and called the Phoenix Furniture Company. A new factory was built for Phoenix on West Fulton and Summer Streets. As the company prospered it produced chamber suites, folding beds, book cases, dining tables, and heavy office furniture for shipment all across the country. By 1880, the company employed an average of 520 people.

After he retired in 1879, William Berkey wrote a book *The Money Question*, and three years later entered the furniture business again by forming the William A. Berkey Furniture Company, to manufacture tables and upholstered furniture. He conducted this business alone until January 1, 1886 when a stock company was organized with William A. Berkey as President, W.H. Jones as vice-President, and L.T. Peck as Secretary - Treasurer. Mr. Jones had been with the Phoenix Furniture Company and Mr. Peck had been Mr. Berkey's accountant since 1881. This firm was subsequently purchased by the John Widdicomb Company.

Borhutz and Diehl & Company
Furniture style: Neo-grec and Renaissance

Borhutz and Diehl & Company were active in the 1870s. Many of their designs were very elaborate.

Charles A. Boudoine
Home address: 718 Fifth Avenue
Business address:
1829 -20, 508 Pearl Street, New York, New York
1849 - 335 Broadway, New York, New York
475 Broadway
Born: 1808 in New York City
Furniture style: Rococo

Charles Boudoine was of French descent and went to France every year. (His wife Ann Postley was milliner before their marriage) He imported French furniture, hardware and upholstery. His own furniture is a restrained, delicate interpretation of Rococo Revival style. He retired in 1856 and invested in real estate in New York. A designer for Boudoine was Mr. Kimbel later of the firm Bembe and Kimbel.

Henry Boyd
Cincinnati, Ohio
Born: 1802 in Kentucky
Furniture style: Rococo

Henry Boyd was born a slave and was bound out to learn cabinetmaking. He bought his freedom in 1826 and moved to Cincinnati. In 1833 he invented and patented a bed-stead, and by 1836 he owned a factory making these beds. His shop made all kinds of furniture and was open until 1862 when, after being burned out three times, the insurance company refused to insure him again so he closed the shop.

Levi C. Boyington
Chicago, Illinois

Levi C. Boyington patented an automatic cabinet folding bed. He sold not only through his Chicago firm but through E.H. Norton in New York.

Thomas Brooks
Brooklyn, New York
Business address:
127-129 Fulton Street
Born: 1811
Died: July 6, 1887 in Dalton, Massachusetts
Furniture styles: Gothic, Rococo and Renaissance

Thomas Brooks was a cabinetmaker working between 1850 and 1870. He exhibited two sideboards at the Crystal Palace that were said to have been designed by Gustave Herter.

1841-42 he is listed in the Brooklyn directories as a partner of Lorenzo Blackstone.

Henry Brunner
New York, New York
Business address:
1840 - 396 Hudson Street
1848 - Brunner and Moore - 174 Fulton Street
1853-54 - 75 & 77 King Street
1876-77 - 41 West 14th Street
Born: 1810 in Prussia
Furniture style: Rococo

Henry Brunner was a cabinetmaker in Germany who emigrated to New York city in 1832. He appears in the New York city directory for 1840-41. In 1846/47 his brother Peter is also listed, but separately.

In 1850 the business lists Henry Brunner, Peter Brunner, and Brunner and Moore. In 1856 Peter retired and in an 1882 *Furniture Gazette* is quoted, "Me and Roux and Hutchings are the only ones of the old fellows left in New York, and Hutchings was in the lumber business in the beginning."

In 1891 the firm was purchased by George C. Flint, and eventually became Flint and Horner.

William Burns
New York, New York
Business address:
1842-1856 - partnership between William Burns and Mr. Trainque
1857-1859 - partnership between brothers William and Thomas Burns

Born: about 1805 in Scotland
Died: April, 13, 1867
Furniture style: Gothic

William Burns came to New York in 1833. He is most famous for his furniture of the Gothic style made while he was in partnership with Mr. Trainque between 1842 and 1856 in New York. Later, he had a partnership with his brother for two years between 1857 and 1859, and from 1860 until 1866 he worked alone.

Richard Byrne
White Plains, New York
Business address:
1833 - Baltimore, Maryland
1842-1845 - Dobbs Ferry, New York
1845-1883 - White Plains, New York
Born: 1805 in Ireland
Died: 1883 in White Plains, New York

Richard Byrne came to the United States from Ireland in 1833 and settled first in Baltimore, Maryland. He moved to Dobbs Ferry, New York and White

Henry Connelly dolphin pedestal card table. *Photograph courtesy of Girard College.*

Plains, New York where he remained. He is associated with Ambrose Wright at Tarrytown, New York about 1850-1866.

Henry Connelly
Philadelphia, Pennsylvania
Business address:
1801 - 16 Chestnut Street
later - 44 Spruce Street
- South Fourth Street
- 8 Library Square (now Sansom Street)
Born: 1769 or 1770
Died: 1826
Furniture style: late Sheraton

Henry Connelly was of Irish extraction and little is known of his early years. He first appears in Philadelphia directories in 1801 as a cabinetmaker. Towards the end of his career he made an Empire style, carved, paw-footed sideboard for Stephen Girard's home. There is a striking similarity in the work of Ephraim Haines' and Henry Connelly's furniture.

Walter Corey
Portland, Maine
Born: 1809 in Ashburnham, Massachusetts

Walter Corey came to Portland, Maine in 1836 and bought out the cabinetmaker Nathaniel Ellsworth. Corey with his friend Jonathan Bancroft revolutionized the way furniture was made in Maine. Bancroft supervised the factory, Corey dealt with customers. They first used horse powered turning lathes, then steam driven. They produced 300-500 chairs a week.

In 1842 Corey acquired water rights at Windham on the Presunpscot River, Windham, and set up a mill. By 1850 sawing, planing and turning of beds was done at Windham, then taken to Portland for assembly.

In 1853 Corey fire-proofed his buildings. In 1860 Bancroft died. Hotels became major buyers of Corey furniture. By 1864 the company produced 15,000 chairs a year. In 1866 the plant was destroyed by fire. Temporary quarters were set up and reorganization begun, and Mr. S. March and D. Rice became partners. In 1870 the Windham operation was closed. The firm never again manufactured in quantity like it did originally. They became known for novelty furniture. In 1889 Corey died. The firm continued as a showroom until 1941.

James W. Cooper
Philadelphia, Pennsylvania
Business address:
1875 - 17th and Washington Avenue

James W. Cooper started in the furniture business in 1850 after leaving the cigar business. He started as a one-man shop and within eighteen months moved to larger quarters. in 1875 he built his own factory at 17th and Washington Avenue where he used a 20-horsepower engine to operate his carving machines and lathes. His shop was organized to facilitate assembly line production.

Daniels and Hutchins
Troy, New York
Business address:
1835 - Albe C. Daniels - 18 Congress Street

1850 - John Hutchins - 199 River Street
1855 - Daniels and Hutchins - 199 River Street
1870 - Albe C. Daniels

Albe C. Daniels
Died: March 20, 1883
John Hutchins
Died: October 9, 1884
Furniture style: Gothic

Albe C. Daniels was listed in 1835 as an established furniture dealer. In 1836-37, he is listed as a cabinetmaker, and by 1840 as having warerooms. This listing continues until 1855 when he is again listed as a cabinetmaker.

John Hutchins was listed in 1845 without an occupation but the following year as a "hammer maker." He is not listed in 1846 or 1848, but reappears in 1850 at 199 River Road as a "cabinet and upholstery" shop.

The 1855 city directory lists Daniels and Hutchins together for the first time as "Furniture and Upholstery Warehouse. All kinds of gilt frames made to order." They made fine examples of Gothic Revival furniture which has descended in the James Miligan family in Saratoga Springs, New York. The firm continued until 1870 when Daniels name alone is given as a cabinetmaker and John Hutchins is listed with Alexander and George H. Wheeler at 860 River Street as "file manufacturers". Hutchins continues to be listed in 1875 and 1880 but with no occupation.

Albert H. Davenport

Boston, Massachusetts
Business address:
Boston Furniture Company - 96-98 Washington Street
Born: 1845 in Malden, Massachusetts
Died: 1906

Albert H. Davenport was the bookkeeper of the Boston Furniture Company from 1866 until he purchased the company in 1880. This was an already prosperous business which Davenport expanded by using exceptional craftsmanship and design for his furniture. He was commissioned to furnish the Throne room at Iolani Palace in Hawaii, and under McKim, Mead and White, his firm made furniture for the White House state dining room in 1902.

In 1916, ten years after Davenport died, the Boston Furniture Company merged with Irving and Casson and subsequently made interiors for churches such as St. Patrick's Cathedral and St. Thomas Cathedral in New York city.

A. J. Davis

Born: 1803
Died: 1897

A.J. Davis was an American architect who sought to create the look of Medieval times, but not necessarily its correctness. He was influenced by the work of Louden and Pugin in England, but he never visited there. Some of Davis's designs were carried out by Richard Byrne and Ambrose Wright. His work is most prominently displayed at Lyndhurst, Tarrytown, New York.

J. Washington Davis
Louisville, Kentucky
Furniture style: Renaissance

J. Washington Davis founded J.W. Davis and Company in 1868 and made fine and medium grade chamber suites. They grew to employ 120 to 175 skilled workmen with all the newest machinery. The company changed its furniture patterns annually to introduce new designs.

A suite of master bedroom furniture which was made by Davis and Company in 1870-71 was sent to the Philadelphia Centennial Fair in 1876 where it won a first place award. At the fair exhibiting his inventions and manufactured farm and saw mill equipment was Mr. T. Brennan who saw, admired, purchased and brought back to Louisville this suite of furniture. It can still be seen today at the Brennan House in Louisville.

J.W. Davis and Company continued in business until 1891 when Mr. Davis either died or left the company.

Julius Dessoir
New York, New York
Business address:
1842-43 - 88 Pitt Street
1843-1845 - 373 Broadway
1846-1851 - 499 Broadway
1852-66 - 543 Broadway
1863-66 - 12 East 18th Street
Furniture style: Rococo

Julius Dessoir's cabinetshop is listed at different locations between 1842-1852. His sons Robert and Herman joined the business about 1859 and from 1860 until 1863 they are listed both separately and as J. Dessoir and Sons at 543 Broadway. From 1863 until 1866 Robert and Herman are listed as cabinetmakers at 12 East 18th Street. The 1866 directory lists the brothers again as R&H Dessoir, at both addresses.

Augustus Eliaers
Boston, Massachusetts
Business address:
1851 - 419 Washington Street
Furniture style: Gothic

Augustus Eliaers was first listed in the Boston directory of 1849. He opened a drawing school with August Gassiot. In 1851, he opened a cabinet shop at 419 Washington Street. In 1853, he was honored for his entries in the Crystal Palace exhibition in New York. He worked through the 1850s and 1860s. His last listing in the Boston directory is in 1865. He was best known for his patent in 1853 for chair/library steps and his flying staircases, and patent pieces like an invalid chair, reclining railroad seat and barber chairs.

C. Flint
New Orleans, Louisiana
Business address:
1834 - 23 Custom Street
1841-1842 - 23 Custom Street and 49 Conti
1843-1858 - 49 Royal
1850 - 46 and 48 Royal

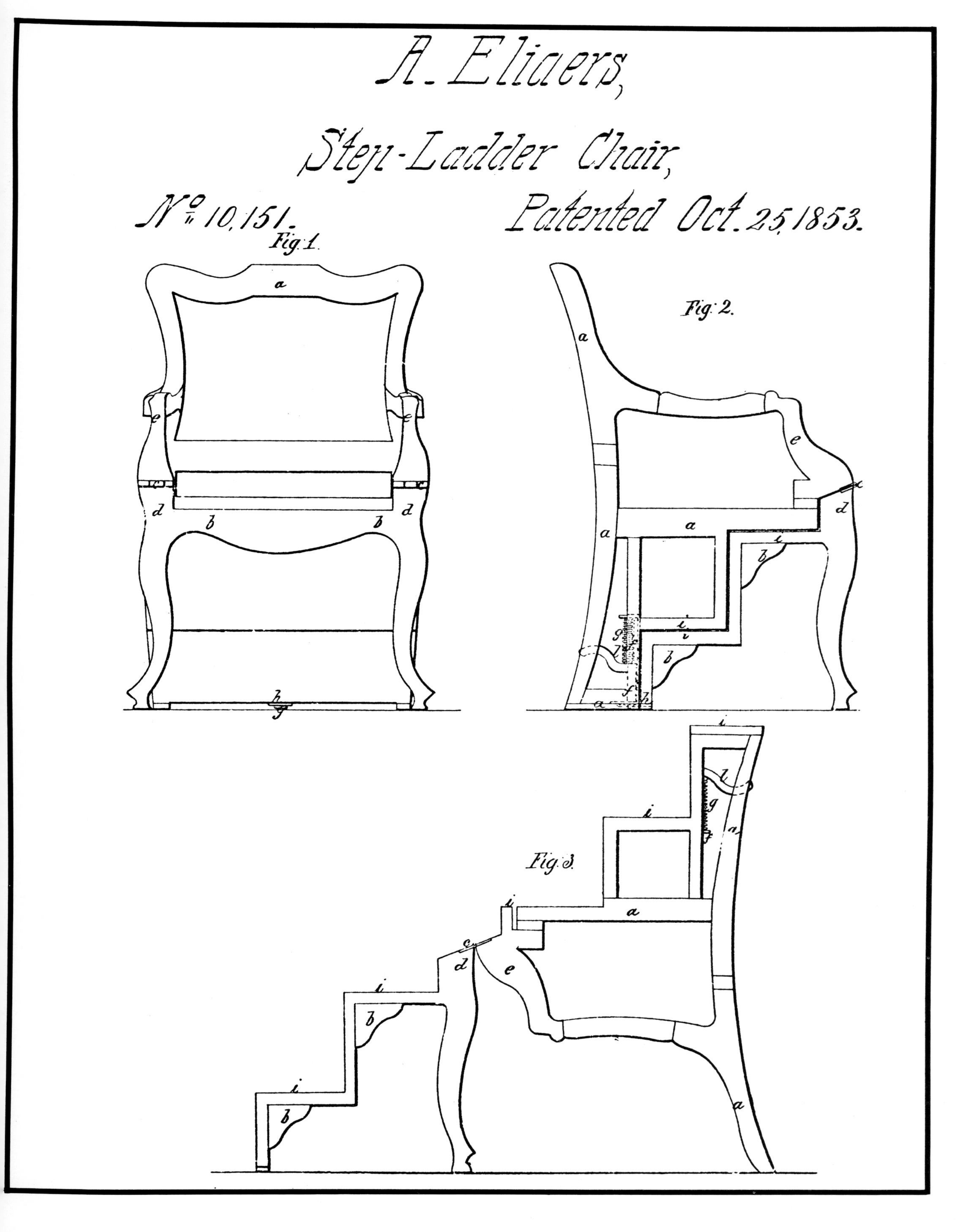
A. Eliaers,
Step-Ladder Chair,
No. 10,151.
Patented Oct. 25, 1853.
Fig. 1.
Fig: 2.
Fig. 3.

Furniture style: Renaissance

The firm of Flint and Carnes is listed in 1834 as a furniture warehouse. That year, John Carnes is listed at 189 Hospital Street with no occupation. The 1838 directory lists C. Flint alone at 23 Custom House with a furniture warehouse, and the 1841 and 1842 directories add another address at 49 Conti to this listing. In 1843, C. Flint is listed at a new location at 49 Royal. That year, James H. Jones is listed at 202 Ichoupitoulas with a furniture store. In the 1846-1858 directory, the firm C. Flint and Jones is listed at 49 Royal. From the 1850 directory until the late 1860s, the entry for C. Flint and Jones lists 46 and 48 Royal. After the Civil War, Robert Mitchells (see Mitchells and Rammelsburg) took over these premises for a branch store known as Mitchells and Craig.

46 NEW ORLEANS DIRECTORY.

FURNITURE.

C. FLINT & JONES,

44 AND 46 ROYAL STREET, NEW ORLEANS,

Would invite the attention of their friends and the public to their

LARGE AND WELL SELECTED STOCK OF CABINET FURNITURE.

Having within the past year greatly enlarged their establishment, they are now enabled to exhibit the best and most varied assortment of Cabinet Furniture ever offered for sale in the South, comprising everything necessary in the furnishing of a dwelling.

IN ADDITION TO FURNITURE, WE KEEP FOR SALE

Plush, Hair Enameled Cloth, Gimp, Cord, Tassels, Springs, Tacks, Twine,

VARNISH, GLUE, &C.

SPRING, HAIR AND MOSS MATTRASSES,

Patent Spring Bed Bottoms,

A NEW AND ECONOMICAL INVENTION,

Comforters, Spreads, Sheets, Pillow Cases and Mosquito Bars.

MIRRORS OF ALL SIZES IN ENDLESS VARIETY.

PLAIN AND CHECKED INDIA MATTING.

REFRIGERATORS

Of all kinds, together with ICE BOXES of every size.

City and Country Purchasers will always find our stock ready for their inspection, and are cordially invited to visit our store and examine for themselves.

Advertisement from the Gardner & Wharton Directory, 1858, page 46.

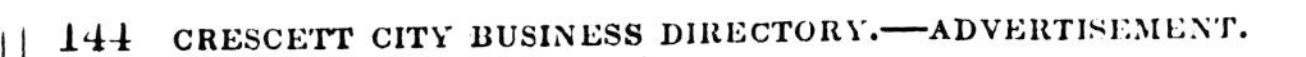

144 CRESCETT CITY BUSINESS DIRECTORY.—ADVERTISEMENT.

C. FLINT & JONES,

DEALERS IN

FURNITURE,

44 AND 46 ROYAL STREET,

NEW ORLEANS.

The subscribers would invite the attention of their friends and purchasers to their large and well selected stock of

CABINET FURNITURE.

Having, within the past year, greatly enlarged their establishment, they are now enabled to exhibit the best and most varied assortment of CABINET FURNITURE, ever offered for sale in the South, comprising everything necessary in the furnishing of a dwelling.

Feathers; Spring, Hair and Moss Mattresses; Varnish, and Bedding of all kinds constantly on hand.

Purchasers from a distance can rely upon their Goods being packed in such a manner as to insure their safety in transportation, and will always find our stock ready for their inspection, and are cordially invited to visit our store and examine for themselves.

☞All orders by mail promptly attended to.

C. FLINT & JONES, 44 and 46 Royal Street,

(ONE SQUARE BELOW THE POST OFFICE.)

Advertisement in the 1858-59 Crescent City Business Directory page 144.

George C. Flint Company
West 23rd Street in New York

George C. Flint Company was the successor to the firm of Henry Bruner. He is first listed in the New York 1894/95 city directory. He worked until 1913. The cabinet at the Metropolitan Museum of Art closely resembles the work of Majorelle the French designer.

Gallier House
1132 Royal Street
New Orleans, Louisiana

This town house was built by architect James Gallier, Jr. between 1857 and 1859. Although none of the original furniture was available for the restoration of the house, an inventory accompanied Mr. Gallier's will and an original floor plan were preserved so that the house could be redecorated and refurnished in the appropriate manner.

Elijah Galusha
Troy, New York
Born: 1804 in Shaftsbury, Vermont
Furniture style: Rococo

Elijah Galusha came to Troy, New York in 1820 and was married to Mary Clark. He first worked in the Sheraton and Empire styles but became best known for his work in the Rococo revival style. In 1836, he took in a fourteen year old apprentice J. Green who later, with a partner named Waterman, took over Mr. Galusha's shop in 1869. Elijah Galusha died in July of 1871.

Frost, Peterson and Company
New York, New York
Furniture style: Gothic

Frost, Peterson and Company were active about 1868-1880 and made a walnut, child-size, perforated veneer rocking chair that is in the Harris County Heritage Society in Houston, Texas. This or a very similar chair was advertised for sale by Gardner and Company of New York in conjunction with the Philadelphia Centennial in 1876.

Gardner and Company
William Gardner
Oliver Gardner
George Gardner
John Gardner
Joseph Gardner
Business address:
1863 - Clarksville, New Jersey (town name changed to Glen Gardner on January 3, 1871)
1874 - 371 Pearl Street and 334 East 61st Street
1879 - 183 Canal Street
Furniture style: Elizabethan

The five Gardner brothers began a business making picture frames about 1863 and were highly successful. By 1868, local competition by Dr. T. Edgar Hunt put their business on the wane, and by 1870 they were no longer making frames. They continued together, however, as George had been granted a number of patents relating to the construction of chairs.

Patent #127,045 issued May 21, 1872, for Patent States describes the 3-ply veneer chair seat made by gluing veneers together so that the fiber of back layer crosses the others at right angles. The patent design attempted to replace cane seating with a cheaper, stronger, and more durable product. Gardner chair seats were perforated in simple designs and was expected to last forever if it were not exposed to moisture for any length of time. The success of the Gardner seats is proven by the establishment of two plants owned by the Gardners in Glen Gardner by 1873.

Offices to market Gardner seats were opened at 110 Bowery in New York City, and agents were contacted in New York and Philadelphia to sell the product. In 1874, William, Oliver, George, and John moved to New York while Joseph remained in New Jersey.

Gardner and Company first appear in New York city in 1874. It had exhibits at various fairs and won many medals and awards.

The Gardner and Company catalog for 1884 shows opera chairs, benches, and platform rocking chairs.

Hutchins and Mabbett were agents for Gardner and Company.

Thomas Godey
Baltimore, Maryland
Business address:
1849 - 54 1/2 Hanover Street
1850 - 54 Hanover Street
Furniture style: Gothic

Thomas Godey was the successor to John Needles in Baltimore. In 1849 Needles & Son were at 54 Hanover Street, and Thomas Godey was at 54 1/2. Needles is not listed in the 1850 directory but Godey appears as successor to John Needles. He is listed at 54 Hanover until 1858. He may have stayed in business until 1890 but at a different address.

Ephraim Haines
Philadelphia, Pennsylvania
Business address:
100 North Water Street
Born: October 23, 1775 in Burlington, New Jersey
Furniture style: Gothic

Ephraim Haines was a member of the Society of Friends who apprenticed to cabinetmaker Daniel Trotter in Philadelphia in 1791. In 1798, he became a partner in Trotter's business, married Trotter's daughter Elizabeth in 1799, and took over Trotter's business in 1800 after Trotter's death. Haines made a suit of parlor furniture for Stephen Girard's home as 21 and 23 Water Street from black ebony Girard had imported. After 1811 he ceased making furniture to operate a mahogany yard. His furniture is similar to that made by Henry Connolly, also of Philadelphia, with a bold bulb above a long turned terminal on his legs.

Hall and Stephens

The firm Hall & Stephens carried the Case "patent folding bed and seatee" that had been patented by Joseph Greenleaf assignor to himself and A.F. Case of New Haven, Connecticut.

E. Haines marble top pier table. *Photograph courtesy of Girard College.*

E. Haines settee. *Photograph courtesy of Girard College.*

Hart, Ware & Company
Boston, Massachusetts
Philadelphia, Pennsylvania
Business address:
1851 - 280 Chestnut Street
1855 - Haley and Ware and Company - 12th Street and Buttonwood.
1856 - Ware and Hall - 215 North 2nd Street
1871 - Hall and Ludwig
after 1871 - Hart, Ware and Company
Furniture style: Elizabethan

Hart, Ware & Company moved to Philadelphia from Boston in 1851. In June 1854, Hart left the firm and Richard Ware joined Jonathan Haley to form Haley and Ware and Company (The company was Thomas Hill and Reuben Haywood). The outlet in Baltimore that Hart & Ware had opened was continued by Haley & Ware until July 1855. In 1855 Haywood left the firm to form a partnership with William Merchant.

In 1855 Haley, Ware & Company moved to 12th Street and Buttonwood. In January of 1856 the firm was dissolved. In February of 1856 Ware formed a partnership with Hall who had been in business since 1846. Ware and Hall were located at 215 North 2nd Street. In July 1856 they sold this store. In the year following they seem to have gone out of business.

George J. Henkels
Philadelphia, Pennsylvania
Business address:
1843 - 371 South 3rd Street
1844-1850 - (six moves)
1850-1857 - 173 Chestnut Street, shop of Crowford Riddle
1857 - 524 Walnut Street
1862 - 809-811 Chestnut Street
1867 - 13th and Chestnut Streets at Fotteral Mansion
Born: Harpers Ferry, West Virginia
Furniture style: Rococo

George J. Henkels first appeared in the Philadelphia business directory in 1843 and occupied various locations during the next seven years. His shop was destroyed by fire in 1854 but he rebuilt at the same site. In 1867, he is listed in partnership with George S. and B. W. Lacy. Henkels retired in 1877 as a widower with thirteen children. His son D. George Henkels bought out his uncle's (John A. Henkels) share of the business and continued the shop. The Henkels shop employed D.M. Karcher and Gustave Grossman who each later became well known cabinetmakers.

George Henkels was a prolific writer against the use of steam powered machinery, advertised frequently, and exhibited in trade fairs in Washington, Boston, and in Philadelphia at the Franklin Institute. He was an exhibitor at the Crystal Palace in 1853 where he showed "relic wood" furniture in the "colonial style" with veneer made from a 200 year-old maple tree in Independence. He also had an exhibit in Philadelphia at the Centennial of 1876.

Mr. Henkels was known for discovering a process to remove acrid oil from walnut wood before the wood was varnished. This process left the walnut with the color and appearance of rosewood and made walnut a more important wood.

Elias Matter

James M. Nelson
Born: 1809 in Milford, Massachusetts
Died: January 18, 1883

Elias Matter
1859 - with C.C. Comstock
1862 - Berkey and Matter with Julius Berkey
1863 - Berkey and Matter with George W. Gay as a partner
1870 - Berkey and Gay when Elias Matter sold his interest to his partners and later bought into Nelson, Comstock & Company to form Nelson, Matter & Company
Furniture style: Renaissance

The furniture company which eventually became the famous Nelson and Matter in Grand Rapids began in 1854 as a partnership between cabinetmaker E.W. Winchester and William Holdane. The following year it was run jointly by brothers E.W. and S.A. Winchester. During the panic of 1857, the brothers convinced C.C. Comstock to take over their plant and he ran it until 1863 when he sold half of the interest to James M. and Ezra T. Nelson. The firm then became Comstock, Nelson & Company.

In 1865, Mr. Comstock gave one fourth of his interest to his son, and sold one eighth interest each to Mr. Colson and Mr. Pugh. The firm then was named Nelson, Comstock & Company.

In 1870, the Comstock interest was purchased by Elias Matter and the firm became Nelson, Matter & Company. Mr. Pugh died in 1870 but his family held his interest until they sold it to the firm in 1872. Mr. Colson died in 1871 and his interest was purchased by Stephen S. Gay in 1872.

In 1878, a third of the Nelson share was sold to a Mr. MacBride and a third to a Mr. Utley. Mr. Gay's share was purchased in 1880 by Nelson, MacBride and Utley. James died in 1883 but his family retained their interest in the firm until 1887.

James M. Nelson's obituary in the February, 1883 *The Michigan Artisan* relates that he came to Grand Rapids in 1826 and that lumbering was his first business. His funeral was at St. Mark's P.E. Church.

dvertisement from the "Michigan rtisan", February, 1891, page 42.

Elias Matter was working in C.C. Comstock's cabinet shop doing piece work in 1859 and later became the shop foreman. He left in 1862 to join a partnership with Julius Berkey (see Berkey write-up) as Berkey and Matter. George W. Gay joined this firm in 1866 and the firm continued until 1870 when Matter sold out to his partners. Later in 1870, Matter bought into Nelson & Comstock Company. Elias Matter revolutionized the selling of furniture in 1862 when he conceived the idea of photo catalogues of furniture rather than taking the furniture itself from city to city for show at trade fairs. Mr. Comstock followed this idea immediately.

The December 1, 1882 issue of *The American Furniture Gazette* announced the opening of a Nelson, Matter & Company branch in Chicago. Messers Knapp, Fuller and Stoddard would head this branch office. Henry I. Hart & Company, upholstery importers from New York, made this branch of Nelson, Matter & Company their Chicago agents.

In February of 1883 the manager of the New York branch of Nelson, Matter & Company was J.W. Wheelock. In March of 1888, Charles Gardner, formerly foreman at Berkey and Gay became the foreman at Nelson, Matter & Company. That year their new warehouse was equipped with the newest in automatic fire extinguishing systems. A series of water pipes connected with the water mains and ran at intervals along the ceiling of each of the eight stories. The pipes had sprinklers which closed by a plug which melted at 155° and permitted a spray to be thrown.

George Norton
Somers, New York

George Norton was a cabinetmaker in Somers, New York between 1830 and 1866.

Daniel Pabst
Philadelphia, Pennsylvania
Business address:
1854 - 22 South Fourth Street
1870 - 269 South Fifth Street
Born: June 11, 1826 in Langenstein, Hesse-Dormstadt, Germany
Died: July 15, 1910
Furniture style: Gothic

Daniel Pabst immigrated to America and settled in Philadelphia by 1849. On July 4, 1854 he opened his own shop at 22 South Fourth Street. Sixteen years later, in 1870, he moved to 269 South Fifth Street and remained there until his retirement in 1896.

Mr. Pabst had strong feelings for Germany. He helped other immigrants, belonged to the German Society in Philadelphia, and wrote and published poetry in German. He married German-born Helena Gross who had seven children. Only three, Emma, Laura, and William, survived to adulthood. The family lived in a row house at 264 South Fifth Street.

Pabst made only the finest furniture and he favored what was known as the "Modern Gothic" style. This was the style promoted by English reformers like Talbert and Dresser. Mr. Pabst took his son William into the business in 1894. Although his last listing is in the 1896 directory, he made furniture for family and friends after his retirement and until his death.

Although ads by Pabst stressed "original design" his famous sideboard seems to have as its source the design book published in 1868 by Henry Carey Baird.

Percier and Fontaine
Paris, France
Business partnership: 1794-1814
Pierre Francois Louis Fontaine
Born: 1762
Died: 1853
Charles Percier
Born: 1764
Died: 1838
Furniture style: Renaissance

The partnership Percier and Fontaine was active between 1794 and 1814. Their work to remodel the Paris mansion of M. de Chauveline came to the attention of Napoleon Bonaparte, after which they were appointed as the leader's architects. As long as their association with Napoleon lasted, they did no private work. Fontaine was the executive partner while Percier was the designer.

August Pottier
New York, New York
Business address:
1853 - Herter, Pottier & Company
1859 - Pottier & Stymus
1871 - Lexington Avenue between 41st and 42nd Streets
1883 - Fifth Avenue at 42nd Street
Born: 1823 in Coul ommiers, France
Died: 1896
Furniture style: Moorish

August Pottier emigrated to New York in 1847 and worked for E.H. Hutchings and Company. By 1853, he exhibited at the London Crystal Palace, and was a partner in the firm of Herter, Pottier and Company. In the late 1850s, Pottier worked for the decorating firm of Rochefort and Skarren where William Stymus also worked. In 1859, Pottier and Stymus took over Rochefort and Skarren. By 1871, they had a factory occupying a full block on Lexington Avenue. In 1872 this location became their showroom as well and was their headquarters. Pottier and Stymus were commended at the Philadelphia Centennial Fair in 1876 for "skillful use of materials, happy blending of colors and ornamentation of the highest order of art". By 1880, a son of each of the founders was active in the firm.

According to the *American Furniture Gazette*, the Pottier & Stymus building at 42nd Street and Fifth Avenue was started in 1882. This building burned on March 1, 1888 with a loss estimated at $200,000 and insurance coverage for $100,000.

The *American Furniture Gazette* of March 15, 1883, states:

> Mr. J.C. Hood, who before he struck it rich in the "Big Bonanza" mine, used to "knock down nickles" as a San Francisco bar tender. He lately paid $5,000 for the bedstead exhibited by Pottier and Stymus Manufacturing Company. The bedstead is a miracle of extravagant taste-

lessness and Mr. Flood is probably the only man in America with enough bad taste and money to buy it. The early education of a saloon keeper is needed to appreciate such a specimen.

Many men who later became famous in their own right worked for the Pottier and Stymus firm. One such man was George A. Schastey. He worked for Pottier and Stymus before forming his own firm in 1873. He exhibited at the Philadelphia Centennial Fair in 1876 and remained in business until 1897. Another former Pottier and Stymus worker who went on to do well Bernard Maybeck.

Robert C. Renwick
Baltimore, Maryland
Furniture style: Gothic

Robert C. Renwick was active between 1837 and 1890. The best known examples of his Gothic Revival furniture can be seen in the First Presbyterian Church on Park and Madison Avenues in Baltimore, Maryland.

Charles Robinson
Rochester, New York
Furniture style: painted chairs

Charles Robinson came to Rochester, New York from Connecticut in 1825 when the Erie Canal was completed. He made chairs and other furniture. By 1858 he was able to mass produce chairs because he supplied the Western House of Refuge with tools and machines and they provided the boys who made the cane and rush seats. He worked until 1878.

Jacque Alexander Roux
New York, New York
Business address:
1848 - 478 and 479 Broadway
Born: March 16, 1813 in France
Furniture style: Gothic, Rococo, Renaissance, Louis XV

Alexander Roux emigrated to New York city where he married three times and had six children. In 1855, he employed 125 people. A set of Renaissance Revival bedroom furniture in the Henry Shaw House at 479-481 Broadway, St. Louis, Missouri which Alexander Roux made dates no later than 1866. This set shows how early he switched from the Rococo style. The height of his success occurred around 1870.

The *American Furniture Gazette* for December 1, 1882 related this about the house of A. Roux at Eighteenth Street in New York city:

"It was a small house, packed so full of superb furniture, that either the customer or a salesman had to stand on the sidewalk when a purchase was being made."

Alexander Roux retired in 1881 but the firm continued under his son until 1898. Roux was cited for fine Louis XV furniture by Andrew Jackson Downing in *The Architecture of Country Houses*.

Henry I. Seymour
Troy, New York

Henry I. Seymour ran a chair factory in Troy, New York form 1851 until 1885. He also held several patents for chair designs.

M. & H. Schrenkeisen
New York, New York
Business address:
23-29 Elizabeth Street
Furniture style: Renaissance and Neo-Grec

M. & H. Schrenkeesen were active in the 1870s and 1880s. They seem to have made middle-range quality furniture for the more moderate group of people. During the 1880s, the firm was the sole agent for the J. Waylan Kimball Company which made embossed leather chairs.

H. N. Siebrecht
New Orleans, Louisiana
Home address: 303 Tulane Avenue
after 1865 - 301 Common
Business address:
before 1863 - 41 Royal
after 1865 - 11 Chartres
1878 - 49 Royal
Born: 1805 in Hesse-Cassel, Germany
Died: August 29, 1890
Furniture style: Rococo

H.N. Siebrecht came to New Orleans about 1826 and opened an upholstery shop. He gradually enlarged his facilities to accommodate his growing furniture and antiques business. His work is characterized by deep carving and solid wood backs to his chairs and sofas. The Civil War seriously disrupted his business but he opened again when it ended.

The 1880 business directory for New Orleans listed his business as H.N. Siebrecht & Company. The 1884 directory lists Samuel Fitzhugh as company

H. N. SIEBRECHT.

ath of the Veteran Upholsterer and Furniture Dealer.

connecting link between the good old ding days of ante bellum, when money was ntiful and business slow but profitable, the active present times in which affairs transacted with a rush and swirl "quick sales and small profits," dropped from the chain of man life. Mr. Henry N. Siebrecht, the eran upholsterer and dealer in furniture, tiques, bric-a-brac, statuary, ancient ses and ornaments, is no more. He depar- this life, last night, at his residence No. Tulane avenue, in the fullness of his 85th ar. He was a native of Hesse- ssel, Germany, and had been a ident of this city for at least y, four years. He was a master of the up- stering business when he settled in the y and he immediately opened a shop. For r three score years he has kept at his rk, succeeding in enlaying his field of opera- ns until he branched out as a dealer in niture and next as a bargainer antiques. His business prospered for many rs, until the unsettling war times came, ing to him forever some of his best cus- ners, ruined by the internecine strife. He con- ued in business at No. 49 Royal street until death, which dispossesses this city of a more an ordinary character,—a tradesman who been the purveyor, in household articles, some of our best families for nearly three nerations.

Mr. Siebrecht was thrice married. His third fe, and three daughters by his first mar- ge, survive him.

N. Siebrecht obituary, Friday, ugust 29, 1890.

21

HENRY SIEBRECHT,

Upholsterer & Furniture Manufacturer,

41 and 43 Royal Street, New Orleans,

Has on hand and makes to order, the NEWEST PATTERNS of Rosewood, Mahogany and Oak Parlor, Dining-Room and Bed-Room FURNITURE; and imports from the best Paris Manufacturers, the NEWEST STYLES of Rose-Wood and Fancy Furniture; has also

A LARGE STOCK OF CURTAIN STUFFS,

Medallion Satin, Brocatels, Silk Damask, Silk and Worsted Damask; Lastings; Cotton Damask, &c.; with a splendid selected stock of Bobbinet and Muslin Curtains.

A GREAT VARIETY OF CURTAIN TRIMMINGS,

VIZ: Rich Silk Gimps, Worsted Gimps, Rich Silk Tassels, of different sizes, Curtain Holders and Fringes; Gilded, Wood, and Brass Window Cornices, Curtain Rods, with Ornaments, &c.

PAPER HANGINGS,

A well-selected and large assortment of the richest Gilt and Velvet Paper Hangings, all kinds of fine Satin Parlor, Bed-Room, Dining-Room and Hall Papers, from the richest to the lowest qualities, with suitable borderings.
N.B.—Curtains are made and put up on the windows, complete, in the newest and most fashionable style.

MOSQUITO BARS, AND ALL KINDS OF BEDDINGS, SPRING MATTRESSES, HAIR AND MOSS MATTRESSES, AND CARPETS MADE TO ORDER AT THE LOWEST PRICES.

manager. He may have been married to one of H.N.'s daughters, since his residence is listed at Siebrecht's home.

Francois Signouret
New Orleans, Louisiana
Business address:
1811 - 25 Royal Street
1822 - 64 Royal Street
1823 - 184 Chartres
1824-53 - 144 Royal
Died: December 25, 1852
Furniture style: Rococo and Louis XV

The grade de frise on Seignouret's gallery was an iron partition to prevent intruders from passing from one house to the next. Of the more than 100 cabinetmakers engaged in New Orleans, in this period, Seignouret was one of the best known for his skill and workmanship. Louisiana Tourist Bulletin, July, 1941.

Francois Signouret is first listed in the New Orleans business directory in 1811 as a "Tapissier, Upholster". He served as a private in Plauche Battalion of the Louisiana Militia during the War of 1812. He purchased property at the present site of 409 Bourbon Street on April 4, 1821 from Lauren M. Sagory.

He was married to Jeanne Marie Descrimes. The 1822 through 1827 directories list Joseph Signouret as an upholsterer. Perhaps this was a brother of Francois.

Francois' brother-in-law Jacques Descrimes apparently joined the firm in 1841 at the age of 35 for he continues to be listed until 1853.

After Francois died, he was still mentioned as a wine merchant. The 1854 directory lists Edward Signouret at 144 Royal continuing his father's upholstery and wine businesses. In 1855, the property at 409 Bourbon Street was sold to one of Francois' heirs Joseph Emile Signouret. From 1855 through 1859, E. Signouret of the firm Cavaroc and Company is listed at 144 Royal. On May 3, 1859, Charles Cavaroc and Emile Signouret purchased the Royal Street property from Jeanne Marie Descrimes for $18,000, then sold it to Orson E. Hall on November 29th.

Mr. Sypher
New York, New York
Business address:
1867 - 558 Broadway

The Sypher firm made furniture in the current "taste of the day" and were well known for their copies of Early American designs, particularly Sheraton chairs and settees.

Jacob Taylor (See also Robert Wood)
New York, New York
Business address:
1808 - 27 Broadway
1811 - Wood and Taylor - in Florida, New York
1820 - Goshen, New York

Jacob Taylor is listed in 1808 as a cabinetmaker in New York city. He moved about 1811 to Florida, New York and formed a partnership with Robert Wood. Their known cabinet work appears in the form of tall clock cases. The 1820 census lists Jacob Taylor living in Goshen, New York (an adjacent town).

William Tillman
Utica, New York
Geneva, New York

William Tillman was a cabinetmaker in Utica, New York in partnership with Eli F. Benjamin between 1822 and 1833. The partnership was dissolved when Tillman moved to Geneva, New York. Tillman and Benjamin were known for their mahogany chairs.

Chalres Tisch
New York, New York
Business address:
1871 - 166 Mott Street
1872 - 164 Mott Street
1886 - 164 Mott Street (workshop) and 14 East 15th Street (showroom)
1889 - 174 Fifth Avenue

Charles Tisch is first listed in New York directories in 1870 as a carver. In 1871 he is listed for chairs, and in 1872 as a cabinetmaker. His advertisement in 1886 lists him as a designer and maker of furniture. His last directory listing is in 1889 as an art dealer.

A cabinet of his was offered to the Metropolitan Museum in New York by Mr. Tisch who said it won first prize at the 1884 New Orleans Exposition.

Edward W. Vail
Worcester, Massachusetts
Business address:
1861 - One Flagg's Block
1864 - 150 Main Street
1877 - Fifteen Union Street

Edward W. Vail is first listed in 1861 as a furniture dealer. By 1864, he was listed as a "patent folding chair dealer" and in 1871 as "patent folding chair manufacturer." He moved his business in 1877 to Union Street where he remained in business until 1891. His Vail Chair Company is believed to have been the largest folding chair business in the country including the stock he exported.

Gotlieb Vollmer
Born: in Wurttemberg, Germany
Died: 1883
Furniture style: Louis XVI

Gotlieb Vollmer came to America in 1830. His first partner in business here was David Klauder in 1843. Between 1845 and 1854, Xavier Montre was his business partner, and thereafter he worked with his son Charles.

Charles Vollmer had been sent to France to learn the furniture business which started as an upholstery shop and expanded to include cabinetmaking. They worked in the tradition of hand crafting.

One of the Vollmers' clients was President James Buchanan who bought one set of furniture for his home "Wheatlands" in Lancaster, Pennsylvania, and another set for the Blue Room of the White House in Washington, D.C.

Cyrus Wakefield
Boston, Massachusetts
Born: 1811 in Roxbury, New Hampshire

Cyrus Wakefield went to Boston in 1826 to help his brother Enoch conduct a grocery business. He saw the rattan used to protect cargo on the Wharves and started selling rattan to basket makers. In 1844 the brothers sold the grocery business and began the Wakefield Rattan Company.

Rattan production was a hand process until Cyrus developed a method for manufacturing. The outside layer of rattan was stripped off and used for cane seats while the inner fiber was used for baskets and skirt hoops. As steel replaced reed for skirt hoops, Cyrus concentrated on the cane for chair seats and utilization of the by-products for floor coverings.

When Cyrus died, his nephew Cyrus Wakefield II took over and expanded the business. In 1888, Cyrus II died and Charles Lang became manager. It was he who consolidated the business with the Heywood brothers in 1897. (See also Heywood Brothers and Company)

Henry Weil
New York, New York
Furniture style: Rococo

Little is known of Henry Weil except the diary of Ernest Hazen, a New York cabinetmaker who wrote "Henry Weil made those ugly heavy veneered, 8-cornered high post bedsteads of which you find so many down South." Hazen, who once worked for Sampson and Keine in New Orleans, claimed that this company was supplied by Henry Weil in New York. Henry Weil sent most of his furniture to New Orleans.

Gilbert D. Whitmore
Boston, Massachusetts
Business address:
346 Washington Street
Furniture style: Gothic

An example of Gilbert D. Whitmore's work is a Gothic child's chair in the collection of the Society for the Preservation of New England Antiquities in Boston.

William Wilmot
Unadilla, New York
Born: 1790 in Danbury, Connecticut
Died: 1849

William Wilmot moved from Danbury, Connecticut to Unadilla, Otsego County, New York in 1810 to become Unadilla's first cabinetmaker. After he died in 1849, he was succeeded in business by his son Daniel W. Wilmot.

Robert Wood
New York, New York
Business address:
1808 - 26 Fayette Street
1811 - Wood and Taylor - in Florida, New York
1820 - Eighth Ward, New York, New York

Robert Wood was a cabinetmaker in New York city in 1808 and moved to Florida, New York around 1811 to form a partnership with Jacob Taylor. Their cabinetwork appears in the form of tall clock cases. By 1820, the census report lists Robert Wood in the Eighth Ward in New York city.

William S. Wooton
Indianapolis, Indiana
Business address:
before 1870 - George A. Grant and Company - Richmond, Indiana
1870 - Wooten Desk Company - Indianapolis, Indiana
Born: May 12, 1835 in Preble County, Ohio
Died: August 26, 1907 in Denver, Colorado
Furniture style: Renaissance

The Reverand William S. Wooton with a grandchild taken in 1889. One of the grandchildren claims that when 'Grandpa was visiting or staying with them, on Sunday, there would be no fun or games played. Mr. Wooton did not allow cooking or baking on Sundays either, only services. He did however like a game of 'Flinch' with the family on Saturday night".

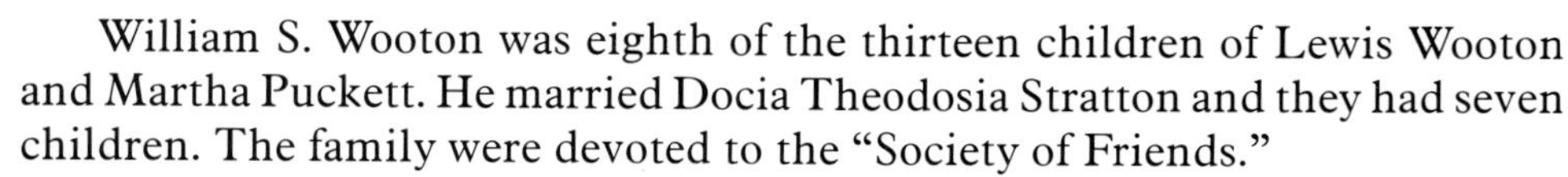

William S. Wooton was eighth of the thirteen children of Lewis Wooton and Martha Puckett. He married Docia Theodosia Stratton and they had seven children. The family were devoted to the "Society of Friends."

Mr. Wooton came to Indianapolis in 1870 from Richmond, Indiana. He had been a partner in George A. Grant and Company a manufacturer of school, office and court furniture. The establishment of the Wooton Desk Company in Indianapolis was recorded in the 1870 census as a manufacturer of school, office, and church desks and furniture.

Wooton and Company were not immediately successful. In 1872 they were awarded the contract for new school furniture only after the first choice concern was unable to fill the agreement.

At the Indiana State Fair in the summer of 1872, William S. Wooton and Company won a five dollar prize for a bookcase and a three dollar prize for a writing desk. The company had also exhibited a five-piece set of office furniture and a collection of school house furniture.

The roots of the Wooton Desk may lie in the history of the period. In the late 1860s this nation had a legacy of the "North's Industrial Machine". The Republican party had adopted the business man and for a half century after the civil war, it continued to nurture him with favorable tariffs, banking, railroad, and immigration legislation. The nation had a bounty of copper, iron, silver, gold, coal, and timber, and limitless free land. It also had a bold group of entrepreneurs like John D. Rockerfeller, Jay Gould, Scribner and Pulitizer and, with the tools available to them, there emerged a combination bound to produce an economic revolution.

The business man, with more than one business to run or an ever expanding business, needed more than his "beaver hat band" to keep track of all his papers. He needed a place for record keeping and record writing. He needed these all in one place, and he needed this to be a secure place. In addition, he wanted some place elegant in order to show his new found status. The Wooton Patent Secretary, "The King of Desks", met all these requirements.

On October 4, 1874 the United States Patent Office issued the patent on what was officially called "Wooton's Patent Cabinet Office Secretary". In November of 1874 Mr. Wooton, John G. Blake and Harmon H. Fuller filed articles of association for the "Wooton Desk Company". In 1876 the firm moved to larger quarters. The patent Secretary was shown at the Philadelphia Centennial Fair in 1876.

The Wooton Desk is based upon Renaissance Revival styling. It is massive, elaborate and rectangular rather than flowing furniture. It uses projecting panels, contrasting woods, gilding, incised lines and turned ornaments. The basic of the desk enabled a person using it to reach 110 compartments without moving his chair. The barrels of the desk swing open, the writing shelf folds up, and there is ledger space that can be reached from a seated position. The desk locks with a single key and on the outside of the left hand door there is a mail slot that can be used for people to leave money or messages when the desk is locked.

The Patent Secretaries made by the company came in four grades: Ordinary, Standard, Extra Grade, and Superior. Each grade could be ordered in three sizes. Prices for the desks ranged from $90 to $750.

The rotary desk was patented in 1876 and also displayed at the Philadelphia Centennial. The desks were commended for compactness, convenience, and utility.

The Rotary desks came in twelve styles, including a single or double pier pedestal, with a flat or slanted writing surface. Rotary desks were made in two grades; Standard and Extra Grade. The prices ranged from $30 to $225.

In the 1876 Indianapolis directory the "Wooton Desk Company" advertised its product as "The King of Desks". The *Furniture Gazette* for August 38, 1875 states, "The Wooton Desk Company has dealers selling its desks in England, Scotland, Canada, Europe, South America and the Far East".

In 1880, the Wootons left Indianapolis and moved to Danville. March 13, 1883 the factory burned with damages of $15,000, $3,000 was covered by insurance and sixty men were temporarily out of work. The last advertisement for the firm appeared August 30, 1884 in

Frank Leslie's *Illustrated Newspaper.*

Mr. Wooton was one of the first leaders of the Danville Friends Meeting which had 100 members by 1885. In 1888, the Wootons moved to Glens Falls, New York where Mr. Wooton was a leader in the Friends Meeting. They continued to work for the meetings founding Ministries until Mr. Wooton died in Denver, Colorado on August 26, 1907. Mrs. Wooton died on November 28, 1908.

Ambrose Wright
Tarrytown, New York
Born: 1794 in England

Ambrose Wright was working in the United States in 1840 when he lived in Hastings, New York. By 1850, he lived in Tarrytown, New York where he was active until 1866. He is associated with Richard Byrne between about 1850 and 1866.

Gothic Furniture

The Gothic furniture in America was an adaptation of Gothic architectural form and ornament. Designs for this type of furniture were first published by Thomas Chippendale in his *Gentlemen and Cabinet Maker's Directory* in 1754. The designs show straight legs, tracery, and chair splats that form pointed arches. The style was encouraged by Andrew Jackson Downing's home in Newburgh, New York and by his two books, *Cottage Residences*, and *Architecture of Country Homes.* Most of the pieces were made of walnut. While this style was not overwhelmingly popular in this country, between 1830 and 1840 it was used by architects and well known cabinetmakers.

Gothic dining room at Lyndhurst, Tarrytown, New York, the summer house of Jay Gould. *Photograph courtesy of the National Trust for Historic Preservation in the United States.*

American Gothic arm chair. *Collection of Lee B. Anderson.* $1000-1500

Carte de Visite by Winder's Photographic Gallery, Cincinnati, Ohio.

Carte de Visite by G.W. Weiser, Steubenville, Ohio.

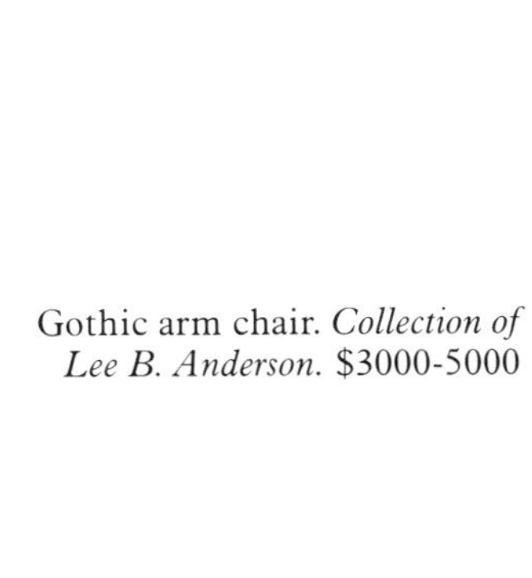

Gothic arm chair. *Collection of Lee B. Anderson.* $3000-5000

Right
American Gothic walnut arm chair, circa 1845. *Photograph courtesy of Sotheby's L.A.* $800-1200

Below Left
Gothic style arm chair. *Photograph courtesy of the Society for the Preservation of New England Antiquities.* $800-1200

Below Right
Gothic style side chair. *Photograph courtesy of the Society for the Preservation of NewEngland Antiquities.* $600-800

John Jelliff Gothic style rosewood slipper chair, circa 1845-55. *Photograph courtesy of The Newark Museum.*

Carte de Visite by an unknown photographer.

Opposite Page
Left: Hall chair by Alexander Roux. Center: Drawing room center table by Alexander Roux. Right: Chair from "Loudoun's Encyclopedia" by A.J. Davis. *Collection of Lee B. Anderson.* $1800-2200

A. Eliaers' stepladder chair. *Photograph courtesy of the Chicago Historical Society.* $3000-5000

Left: Arm chair made by Burns and Tranque from Lyons House in White Plains. Design by A.J. Davis. Center: Mahogany center table by John and Joseph Meeks. Circa 1836. Right: Chair attributed to Alexander Roux. Design drawing from Downing's book. *Collection of Lee B. Anderson.* L-R: $2000-2500, $3000-5000, $800-1200

Marble top, mahogany library table by J. and J.W. Meeks. Table legs are bronze. Couch in background possibly by J. and J.W. Meeks. *Collection of Lee B. Anderson.* $4000-6000

Mahogany tilt top tea table by Alexander Roux. *Collection of Lee B. Anderson.* $3000-5000

Gothic dining table designed by Alexander Jackson Davis for John J. Herrick's Villa "Ericston". *Photograph courtesy of the Lyndhurst Corporation.* $4000-6000

Marble top, mahogany center table stamped J. and J.W. Meeks. Circa 1836-47. *Collection Lee B. Anderson.*

Bench of ebonized oak by Alexander Roux. Designed by A.J. Davis for Lyons House in White Plains. *Collection of Lee B. Anderson.* $3000-5000

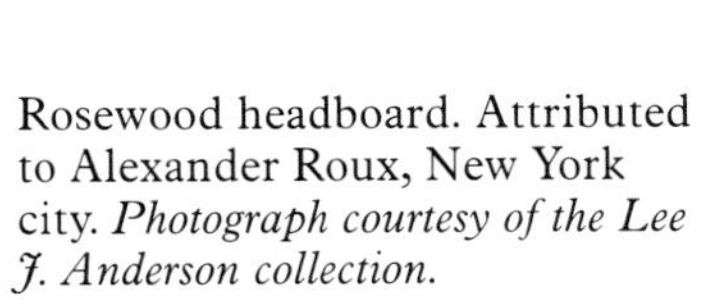

Rosewood headboard. Attributed to Alexander Roux, New York city. *Photograph courtesy of the Lee J. Anderson collection.*

Bed designed by A.J. Davis for Herrick Castle. Made by Burns and Tranque. *Collection of Lee B. Anderson.* $4000-5000

Mahogany hanging shelves by John and Joseph W. Meeks. *Collection of Lee B. Anderson.* $400-600

Rosewood etager attributed to J. and J. Meeks. *Photograph courtesy of Sotheby Parke Bernet.* $4000-6000

Rococo Furniture

American Rococo furniture of the 1840s to 1860s regenerated the cabriole leg, the S-and C-scrolls, and the naturalistic carvings of fruit, birds, flowers and human busts. The rear legs were generally chamfered. Rococo overwhelmingly overtook classical decoration in popularity. The universal acceptance of Rococo styling can be gauged by the fact that it has a specific name in most languages; *Neo barocco* and *Zweite Rokoko.*

Rococo was never favored by architects or designers, it was essentially a decorators style.

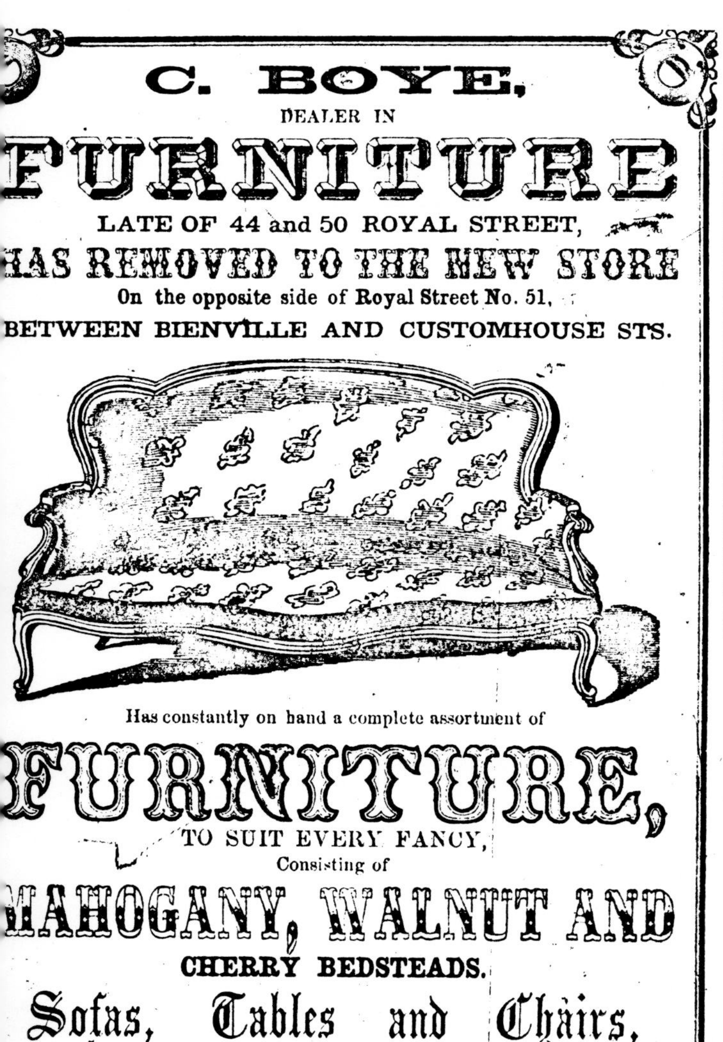

Too often newspapers or handbills have been used to attribute particular pieces of furniture to a single cabinetmaker. The following ads would indicate that the cuts belonged to the printer or publisher and were used indiscriminately as decorations. C. Boye of New Orleans used a couch in his ads that is identical, even to the fabric, to the couch in the Mallard ad.

Left
Boye also advertised using a cut of a bed that is most often attributed to Mallard.

Below
P. Mallard used a dressing table, secretary and cabinet desk a number of his ads and The Southern Furniture Ware-Rooms used the identical cuts.

Opposite Page
J.T. Pidwell in San Francisco used the same cut as P. Mallar and The Southern Furniture Ware-Rooms. The order in which the pieces appear is not even changed.

C. BOYE,

DEALER IN

FURNITURE,

Late of 44 & 50 Royal st., has removed to the new store on the opposite side of

ROYAL ST. No. 51,

BETWEEN BIENVILLE AND CUSTOMHOUSE STS

Has constantly on hand a complete

to suit every fancy, consisting of

Mahogany,

WALNUT

AND

CHERRY

BEDSTEADS.

Sofas, Tables and Chairs,

ARMOIRS, &C., &C.

Which are offered to purchasers on as reasonable terms as at any other establishment in the city.

SOUTHERN

Furniture Ware-Rooms

CHAS. A. STEWART,

DEALER IN

Cabinet Furniture of every Description

And of the latest and most fashionable styles,

LOOKING GLASSES

SPRING, HAIR, AND MOSS

MATTRASSES, MATTING, &C.,

No.'s 171 and 173 Canal street.

Posters and Show Bills, Printed at the Delta Job Office, 76 Camp.

222 SAN FRANCISCO [P] DIRECTORY.

FURNITURE WAREROOMS,

No. 140 WASHINGTON STREET.

J. T. PIDWELL

IMPORTER AND GENERAL DEALER IN

FURNITURE,

BEDDING, LOOKING GLASSES, &c.

Is constantly receiving fresh supplies, and is now prepared to sell at greatly reduced prices. Ladies and Gentlemen furnishing their Houses and Offices will find it to their advantage to call at 140 Washington Street.

He offers for sale that curiosity and "piece of economy," which was on exhibition at the Mechanic's Fair in this City,

PLYMTON'S PATENT SECRETARY BED.

Also, by late arrivals, a few of those justly celebrated

PIANOS!

Manufactured by JAMES W. VOSE, of Boston, and which are now taking precedence of all other Manufacturers, evidenced by the many Prize Medals awarded Mr. Vose. All Pianos warranted to give satisfaction.

ALSO,

CAHART & NEEDHAM'S PATENT AND AUSTIN'S MELODEONS,

Which will be sold cheap for cash, and a liberal discount given to Churches and Sabbath Schools, and to Music Teachers.

BUCKLEY'S FURNITURE POLISH,

Constantly on hand. This to Housekeepers and Furniture Dealers is invaluable. A small quantity of it produces effects truly astonishing.

Armed side chairs by Elija Galusha. *Photograph courtesy of the Rensselaer County Historical Society.*

Sofa and chair by Elija Galusha. *Photograph courtesy of the Rensselaer County Historical Society.*

Room setting showing J. H. Belter parlor suite. Note the unusual paw feet on furniture. Center table is by Meeks. *Photograph courtesy of the Paine Art Center and Arboretum, Oshkosh, Wisconsin.*

"Fountain Elms" pattern arm chair, "Cornucopia" pattern sofa, and pierced, laminated table by John H. Belter. *Photograph courtesy of Sotheby Parke Bernet.* L-R: $15,000-25,000, $50,000+, $50,000+

John H. Belter sofa and four side chairs. Note round seats. *Photograph courtesy of Sotheby Parke Bernet.* $50,000+ (suite).

John H. Belter laminated, pierced, carved "Cornucopia" pattern love seat and side chairs. Center turtle top table attributed to John H. Belter. Note: Small Belter etagere on left. *Photograph courtesy of The Service Collection.* $50,000+ (suite).

John H. Belter laminated rosewood lamp table of unusual size with round marble top. On right; "Fountain Elms" pattern arm chair, on left; "Cornucopia" side chair. Rear etagere is by John H. Belter with cupids, roses and butterflies as decoration. *Photograph courtesy of The Service Collection.*

Close up of cresting on John H. Belter "Cornucopia" side chair. *Photograph courtesy of The Service Collection.* $10,000-15,000

Room setting of John Henry Belter furniture. *Photograph courtesy of the Metropolitan Museum of Art.* $50,000+ (suite).

Left
John H. Belter pierced and laminated rosewood arm chair in the "Fountain Elms" pattern. *Photograph courtesy of the Museum of the City of New York.* $15,000-20,000

Right
J.H. Belter arm chair in the "Fountail Elms" pattern. *Photograph courtesy of the Metropolitan Museum of Art.* $15,000-20,000

Couch attributed to J.H. Belter similar to ones in the Virginia Museum and the Metropolitan Museum of Art. *Photograph courtesy of R. & E. Dubrow.* $8000-12,000

Room setting of John Henry Belter furniture. *Photograph courtesy of the Metropolitan Museum of Art.* $50,000 (suite).

"Tuthill King" pattern John H. Belter Tête-à-tête. *Photograph courtesy of Metropolitan Museum of Art.* $30,000-40,000

Above: "Fountain Elms" or "Arabasket" pattern 3-piece John H. Belter Parlor Suite. Collection of Mr. and Mrs. J. Mello. *Photograph courtesy of Mortons Auction Exchange.* $50,000+ (suite).

Below: "Fountain Elms" pattern John H. Belter arm chairs - 3, and side chair - 1. *Photograph courtesy of Mortons Auction Exchange.* $50,000 (suite).

John H. Belter pierced and laminated Tutthill King pattern marble top table carved with busts of Benjamin Franklin and George Washington. *Photograph courtesy of the Chicago Historical Society.* $40,000-50,000

John H. Belter Tutthill King pattern pierced and laminated piano stool. *Photograph courtesy of the Chicago Historical Society.* $10,000-15,000

Above
Side chairs en suite. *Photograph courtesy of Richard Bourne Auctions.* $2000-3000 ea.

Right
Arm chairs en suite. *Photograph courtesy of Richard Bourne Auctions.* $4000-6000 ea.

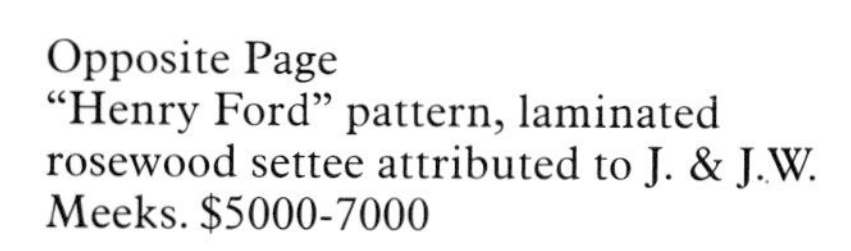

Opposite Page
"Henry Ford" pattern, laminated rosewood settee attributed to J. & J.W. Meeks. $5000-7000

"Rosalie", Natchez, Mississippi. *Photograph courtesy of Rosalie.*

Turtle top "Rosalie" pattern table. Note all carved heads are different. *Photograph courtesy of R. & E. Dubrow.* $20,000-30,000

"Rosalie" pattern John H. Belter arm and side chair. *Photograph courtesy of Sotheby Parke Bernet.* L-R: $3000-5000, $2000-3000

Left
This view of the chair back shows John Henry Belter's improved method of making a chair back bent along two planes. *Photograph courtesy of the Smithsonian Institution.*

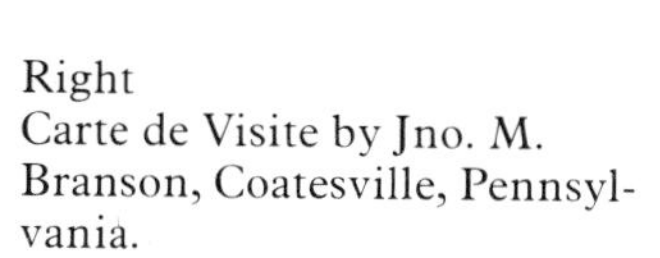

Right
Carte de Visite by Jno. M. Branson, Coatesville, Pennsylvania.

John H. Belter sofa, laminated rosewood in the "Rosalie" pattern. *Photograph courtesy of R. & E. Dubrow.* $6000-8000

Room setting with "Rosalie" arm chair by John H. Belter. Ladies' writing desk very similar to that shown in both the Mallard and the Boye advertisements. *Photograph courtesy of Samuel Dornsife.*

W. & J. ALLEN'S

Cabinet, Chair & Sofa Warerooms

136 SOUTH SECOND STREET, ABOVE SPRUCE,

PHILADELPHIA.

Every article of CABINET WORK constantly on hand, of the most beautiful style and finish.
The attention of MERCHANTS, and of all others desiring well made Furniture, is invited.

W. & J. Allen's warerooms. *Photograph courtesy of the Campbell Collection, Vo. 82, Historical Society of Pennsylvania.*

Arm chairs and side chairs from the parlor set in the Arnot house. *Photograph courtesy of the Arnot Art Museum.* $2000-3000 (suite).

Laminated parlor set by George Henkels of Philadelphia.
Photograph courtesy of Morton's Auction. $3000-5000

G. Henkels arms chair, Philadelphia.
Photograph courtesy of R. & E. Dubrow.
$600-800

From "Technological Innovation and the Decorative Arts" Hagley Museum and Winterthur Museum, Wilmington, Delaware 1973, page 8.

CENTENNIAL SOFA BED—Price, $35 00.

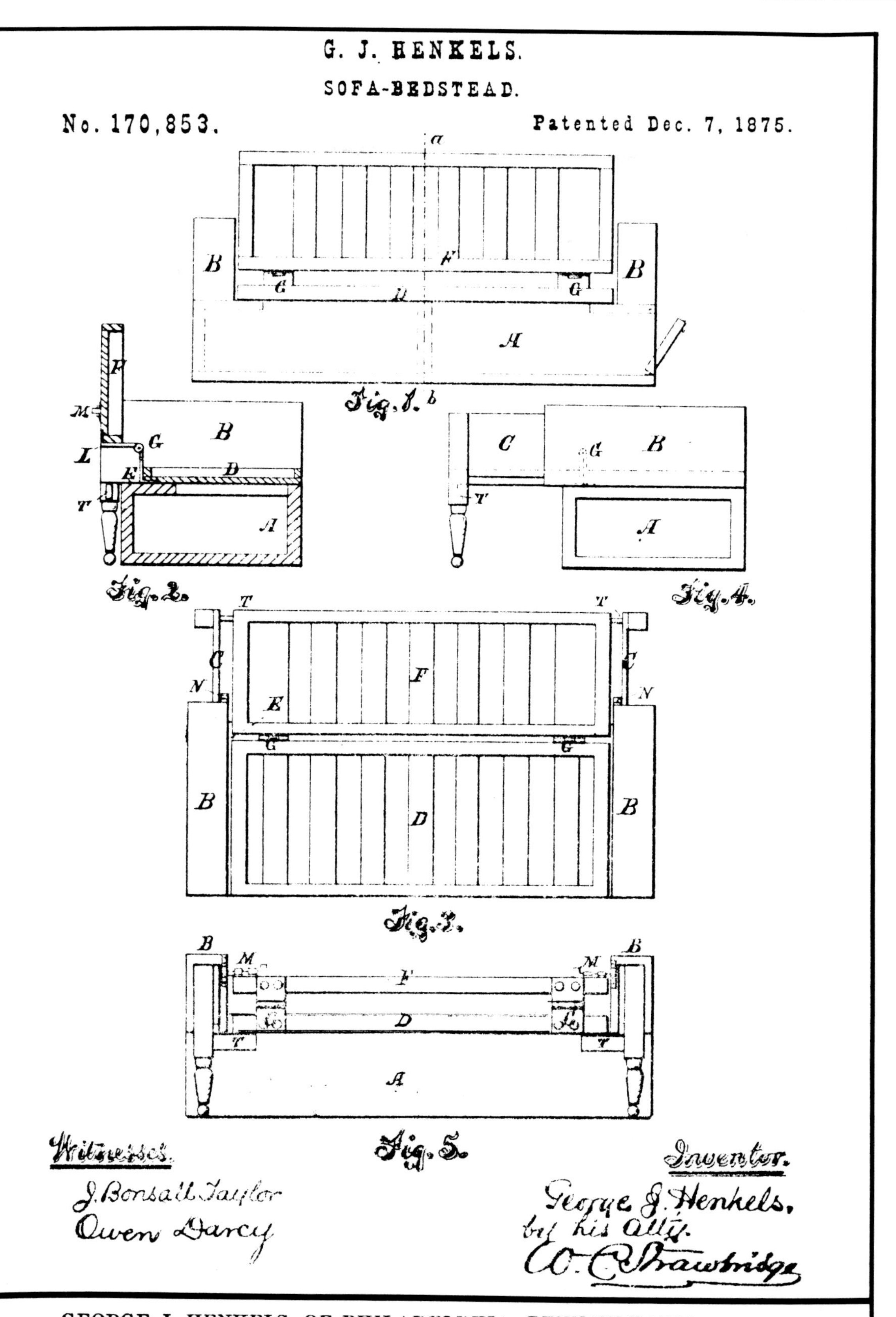

GEORGE J. HENKELS, OF PHILADELPHIA, PENNSYLVANIA

IMPROVEMENT IN SOFA-BEDSTEADS.

Specification forming part of Letters Patent No. **170,853**, dated December 7, 1875; application filed September 23, 1875.

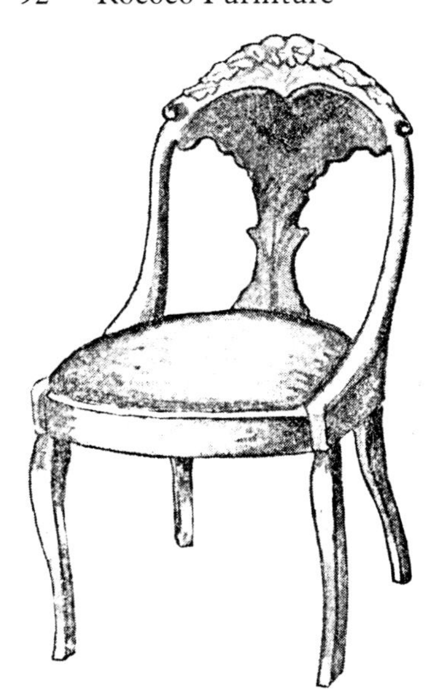

This is the chair traditionally attributed to Francois Seignouret as the "Gondola chair". We were unable to find any documented example of the chair. *Louisiana Tourist Bulletin. July 1941.*

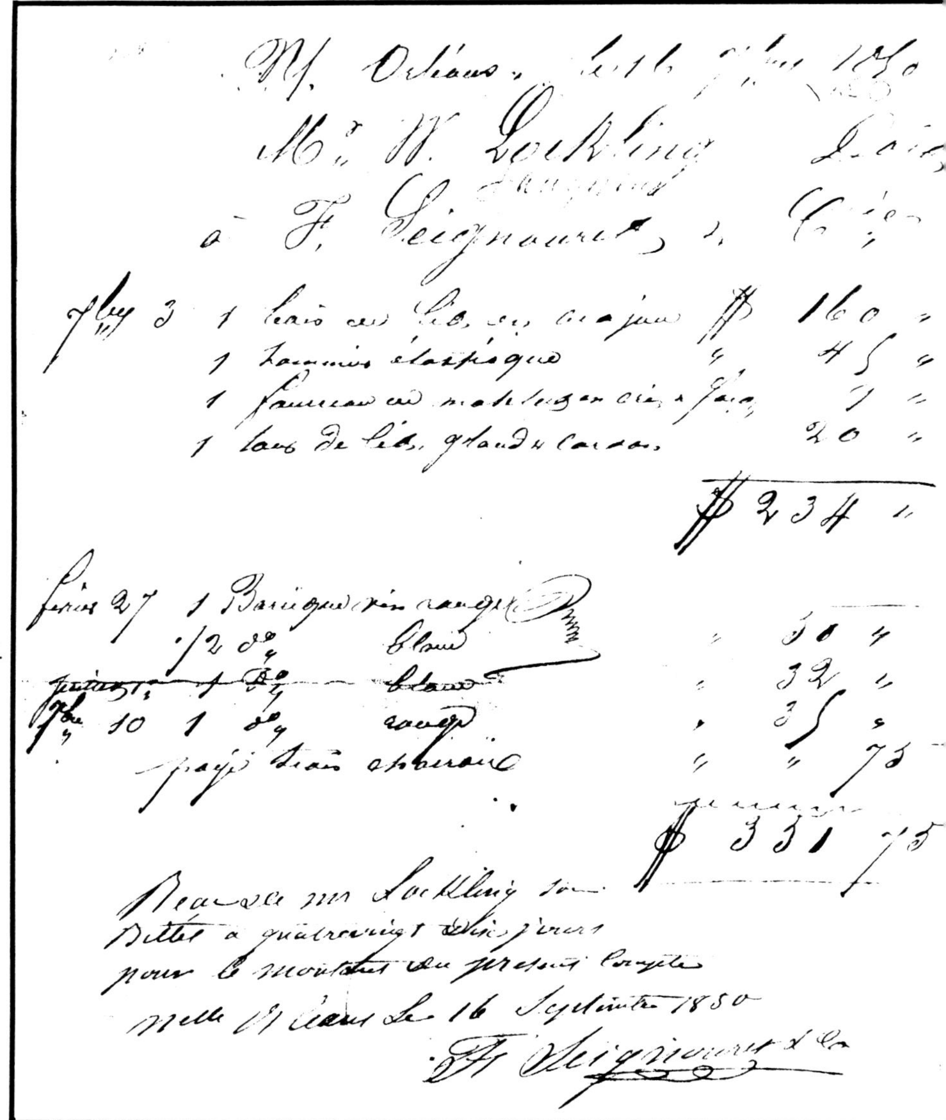

N. Orléans, le 16 7bre 1850

Mr. W. Lockling

à F. Seignouret & Co.

$ 234

$ 331 75

Reçu de Mr Lockling ... pour le montant du présent compte

N. Orléans le 16 Septembre 1850

F. Seignouret & Co

Side chair from a parlor set by Charles A. Boudoine, circa 1852. *Photograph courtesy of the Munson-Williams-Proctor Institute. Proctor Collection.* $1500-2500

Label from the Charles A. Boudoine ladies' writing desk. *Photograph courtesy of the Museum of Fine Arts, Boston.*

Carte de Visite by Jno. M. Branson, Coatesville, Pennsylvania.

Arm chair from a parlor set by Charles A. Boudoine, circa 1852. *Photograph courtesy of the Munson-Williams-Proctor Institute. Proctor Collection.* $2500-3500

Rococo revival slipper chair. $1000-1500

Ambertype showing slipper chair used as a photographers prop.

Period ambertype showing a lady with a Rococo Revival slipper chair. *Collection of R & E. Dubrow.*

Rococo Revival dining chair in the same pattern as slipper chair. $1000-1500

Above
Arm, and side chair in the "Bird" pattern. Note: This set differs from the set in Bayou Bend in the carving on the legs and the hanging grapes. *Photograph courtesy of the Smithsonian Institution.* L-R: $3000-5000, $6000-7000

Left
Laminated rosewood child's chair. Maker unknown. *Photograph courtesy of Service Collection.* $600-800

Right
John H. Belter pierced and laminated child's arm chair. *Photograph courtesy of the Museum of the City of New York.* $3000-5000

Left
Laminated "Shield back" arm chair by John H. Belter. $1000-1500

Below
Laminated rosewood arm and side chair by J.H. Belter. Pattern is known as "Rosalie Without The Grapes". L-R: $3000-5000, $1000-1500

Side chair by John H. Belter in a variation of the "Henry Clay" pattern. Note the round set. *Photograph courtesy of R. & E. Dubrow. Collection of Gallier House.* $2000-3000

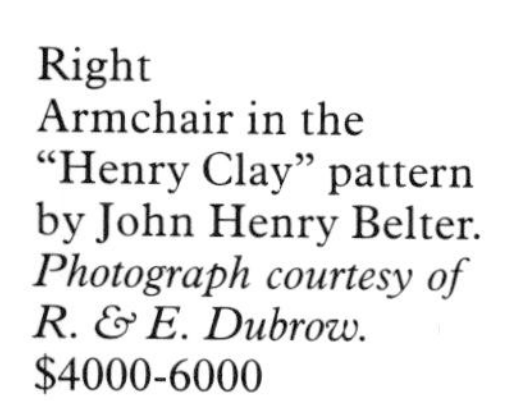

Right
Armchair in the "Henry Clay" pattern by John Henry Belter. *Photograph courtesy of R. & E. Dubrow.* $4000-6000

Left
"Henry Clay" pattern John Henry Belter arm chair. *Photograph courtesy of the New York Historical Society - Fennimore Cooper House.* $2000-3000

"Henry Clay" pattern side chair by John H. Belter. *Photograph courtesy of the New York Historical Society - Fennimore Cooper House.* $1500-2500

"Henry Clay" pattern John H. Belter side chair. *Photograph courtesy of R. & E. Dubrow.* $2000-3000

Laminated rosewood side chair attributed to J. & J. Meeks in the "Hawkins" pattern. $2000-3000

Laminated, pierced rosewood arm chair attributed to J. & J. Meeks in the "Stanton Hall" pattern. *Photograph courtesy of R. & E. Dubrow.* $3000-5000

Meeks "Stanton Hall" pattern arm chair. Note the variation of incised decoration on arms and trumpet legs. *Photograph courtesy of Mrs. S. Crawford.* $2500-4500

Side chair en suite in "Stanton Hall" pattern by the Meeks Company. $15,000-25,000

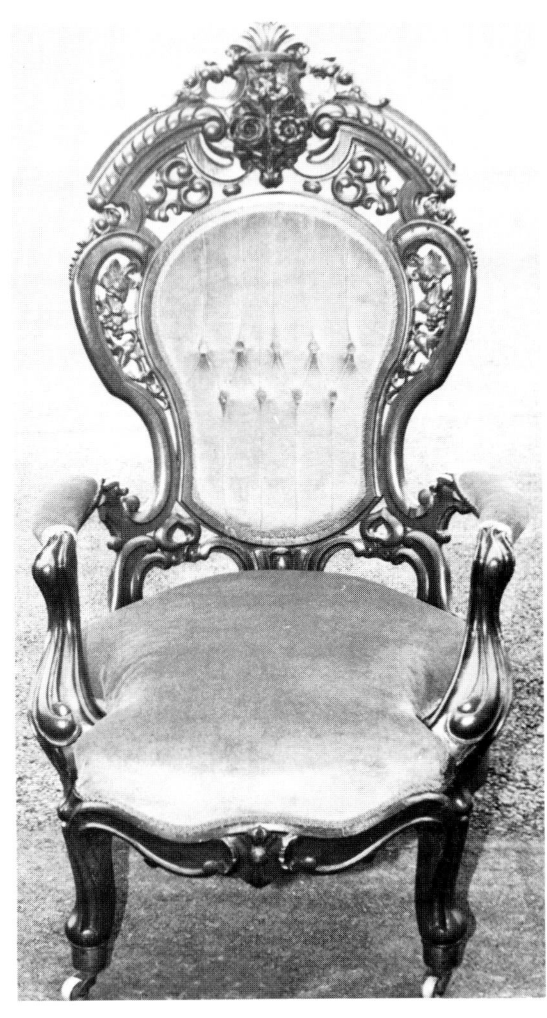

Right
Arm chair en suite. "Henry Ford" attributed to Meeks. *Photograph courtesy of R. & E. Dubrow.* $4000-6000

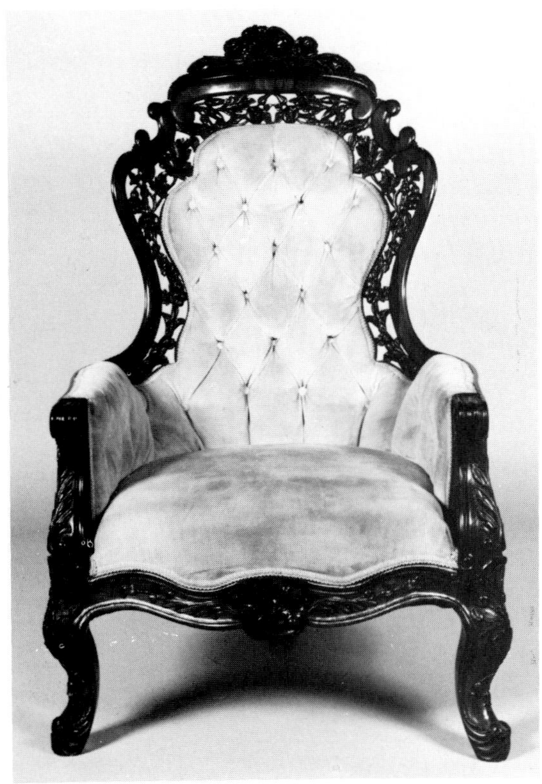

Left
Three-legged corner chair attributed to John H. Belter. *Photograph courtesy of Sotheby Parke Bernet.* $5000-7000

Back of chair.

Arm chair in "Tutthill King" pattern. *Photograph courtesy of Belle Meade Mansion.* $10,000-15,000

Carte de Visite by J. Raine of Richmond.

Special order side chair in the "Tutthill King" pattern. *Photograph courtesy of R. & E. Dubrow.* $6000-8000

Friedrich Springmeier

To

Ida Dusing

Bill of Sale.

Dated, May 23rd 1895

SCHEDULE OF FOREGOING BILL OF SALE.

1, one Piano (Square)
2, one Bedstead
3, one Bureau
4, one Wardrobe
5, 12 chairs
6, 1 round Table
7, 1 square Table

Bill of Sale.—138. John Polhemus Printing Co., Printers and Mf'g Stationers, 121 Fulton St., N. Y.

Know all Men by these Presents,

THAT I, Friedrich Springmeier of the City of Long Island City, Queens County of New York party of the first part, for and in consideration of the sum of One Dollar ($1.00) lawful money of the United States, to me in hand paid, at or before the ensealing and delivery of these presents, by Ida Dusing of the same place party of the second part, the receipt whereof is hereby acknowledged, have bargained and sold, and by these presents do grant and convey unto the said party of the second part, her executors, administrators and assigns, All that certain Piano and Household furniture, located now in the two story frame Dwelling house situated number 410 Rouwenhoven Street Long Island City N.Y.

To have and to hold the same unto the said party of the second part, her executors, administrators and assigns forever. And I do, for my heirs, executors and administrators, covenant and agree to and with the said party of the second part, to warrant and defend the sale of the said Piano and Household furniture hereby sold unto the said party of the second part, her executors, administrators and assigns, against all and every person and persons whomsoever.

In Witness whereof, I have hereunto set my hand and seal this twenty third day of May one thousand eight hundred and ninety five

Sealed and Delivered in the Presence of

Emil Sauermilch

Frederick Springmeier

Bill of sale from Frederick Springmeier to his daughter Ida covering the next three chairs.

This "dish back" chair is one of only five known and is the only one that is documented as descending in the Springmeier family. The Springmeiers were partners and a brother-in-law to Belter. Belter was married to their sister Louisa. Belter's application for patent 23, 1858 covering his chair was twice rejected. Once on the basis that the principles for bending were known and also on the basis of Belter's other patents. The patent office also referred to how close it was to a sounding board patented by a Mr. Bogand in 1857. A third application to the patent office by Mr. Belter together with affidavits by Charles Hogg, George Hulton and Mr. Springmeier finally got the patent granted. $3000-4000

THE METROPOLITAN MUSEUM OF ART
NEW YORK, 28, N.Y.

CABLE ADDRESS
METMUSART

DEPARTMENT OF THE AMERICAN WING

February 1, 1945

Dear Mrs. Dusing,

I have been interested in John Henry Belter and his work for a long time. In 1934 we had an exhibition here and borrowed from Mrs. Edward M. Foote some fine pieces which Belter had made for her grandmother.

I recently saw Mrs. Foote and she told me that following the exhibition she visited you in Kerhonkson and that you might be able to answer several questions about Belter and his partner Springmeyer. Could you tell me how long Springmeyer worked with Belter, and if he too came from Germany and if so, when? In fact, I would like to know all I can about Belter and Springmeyer, as I wish to publish it with pictures of their work very soon.

Mrs. Foote showed me a picture of an armchair which you owned of Belter's. Do you still have this, and if so, would you consider selling it?

Mr. Fritz Foord who is a friend of mine and lives in Kerhonkson in the summer told me recently that he thought you were still living there, and I hope it will not be too much trouble for you to answer all of my questions. It will be a great favor to hear anything you may tell me. I know it is a nuisance to write letters and I am enclosing a stamped envelope, and if you wish to do so, use the back of this letter for your reply.

Hoping to have the pleasure of hearing from you, I am

Sincerely yours,

Joseph Downs

Joseph Downs
Curator

Mrs. William Dusing
Kerhonkson, New York

THE METROPOLITAN MUSEUM
OF ART
NEW YORK 28, N. Y.

NEW YORK, N.Y.
FEB 10
3-PM
1945

Mrs. William Dusing
Kerhonkson, New York

Original letter dated 1945 from Joseph Downs, then curator of the American wing of the Metropolitan Museum of Art, regarding the chair that descended in the family. Mr. Downs used a photograph of this chair in an article in "Antiques Magazine" in 1948. It is addressed to Mrs. I. Dusing, Mr. Frederick Springmeier's daughter.

Original covering from the "Tutthill King" chair that descended in the Springmeier family.

"Tutthill King" pattern arm chair that descended in the Springmeier family. This chair was made by John H. Belter. $20,000-30,000

Third chair descended in the Springmeier family made in the Belter shop. $800-1200

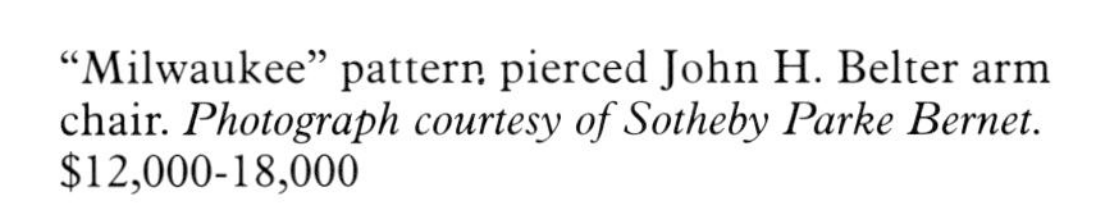

"Milwaukee" pattern pierced John H. Belter arm chair. *Photograph courtesy of Sotheby Parke Bernet.* $12,000-18,000

John H. Belter laminated rosewood slipper chair. *Photograph courtesy of R. & E. Dubrow.* $2000-3000

John H. Belter slipper chair. $2000-3000

Pair of pierced, laminated rosewood slipper chairs by John H. Belter. $6000-8000 pr.

Detail of crest on above chairs. *Photograph courtesy of the Service Collection.*

Above
John Henry Belter slipper chair. *Photograph courtesy of the Metropolitan Museum of Art.* $15,000-20,000

Center
"Fountain Elms" pattern pair of John H. Belter slipper chairs. *Photograph courtesy of W. Watkins.* $5000-7000

Right
Laminated pierced slipper chair by John Henry Belter. Note original gilding on knees. *Photograph courtesy of J. Mello.* $2000-3000

Laminated rosewood side chairs by John H. Belter with carved portrait busts probably Virgil, Chaucer, Dante and Homer. *Photograph courtesy of R. & E. Dubrow. Collection of Gloria and Richard Manney.* 15,000-20,000 (suite; also includes page 111, bottom.)

Carving on set, probably Chaucer.

Carving on set, probably Dante.

Carving on set, probably Virgil.

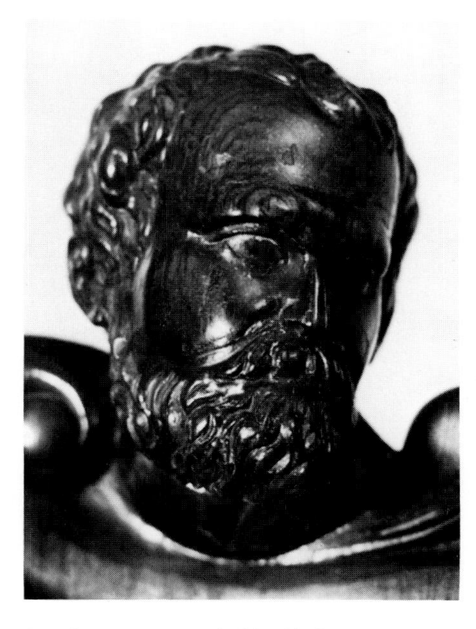

Carving on set, probably Shakespeare.

Carving on set, probably Milton.

Pair of laminated rosewood recamiers by John H. Belter with carved portrait busts probably of Shakespeare and Milton. *Photograph courtesy of R. & E. Dubrow. Collection of Gloria and Richard Manney.*

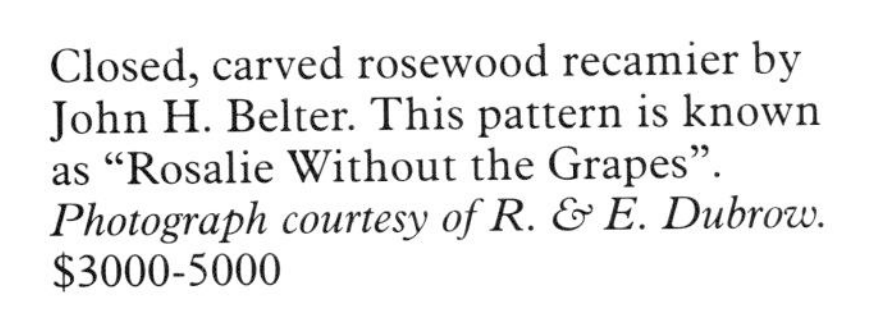

Closed, carved rosewood recamier by John H. Belter. This pattern is known as "Rosalie Without the Grapes". *Photograph courtesy of R. & E. Dubrow.* $3000-5000

Recamier laminated, pierced, rosewood in the "Stanton Hall" pattern. Attributed to J. & J. Meeks. $3000-5000

Recamier by John Henry Belter in the "Henry Clay" pattern. *Photograph courtesy of R. & E. Dubrow.* $2500-3500

"Henry Clay" pattern John H. Belter recamier. *Photograph courtesy of the New York State Historical Association.* $4000-6000

John H. Belter "Fountain Elms" pattern recamier. Laminated rosewood. *Photograph courtesy of the Service Collection.* $18,000-22,000

"Rosalie" pattern John H. Belter recamiers - a pair. *Photograph courtesy of R. & E. Dubrow.* $8000-12,000

John Henry Belter "Fountain Elms" pattern recamier. *Photograph courtesy of Dr. Milton Brindley.* $20,000-25,000

"Tuthill King" recamiers by J.H. Belter, a matched pair, in the Morris Butler House. $35,000-45,000

Settee from a laminated parlor set in the Rococo style. The cabinetmaker has not been identified, but this set was among the original furnishings in the Arnot house which was built in 1833. *Photograph courtesy of the Arnot Art Museum.* $2000-3000

Settee from a parlor set by Charles A. Boudoine, circa 1852. *Photograph courtesy of the Munson-Williams-Proctor Institute. Proctor Collection.* $2000-3000

John H. Belter couch in the "Rosalie Without the Grapes" pattern. Ima Hog Plantation. *Photograph courtesy of the Texas Wildlife Foundation.* $3000-5000

Sofa by Charles Boudoine. *Photograph courtesy of the Art Institute of Chicago.* $5000-7000

Pierced, laminated rosewood love seat in the "Henry Ford" pattern. Attributed to J. & J. Meeks. *Photograph courtesy of R. & E. Dubrow.* $6000-8000

Sofa by J. & J. Meeks in the "Stanton Hall" pattern. *Photograph courtesy of R. & E. Dubrow.* $3000-5000

Sofa in the "Bird" pattern. Note: This set differs from the set in Bayou Bend in the carving on the legs and the hanging grapes. *Photograph courtesy of the Smithsonian Institution.* $10,000-15,000

Sofa by John Henry Belter in the "Henry Clay" pattern. *Photograph courtesy of R. & E. Dubrow.* $3000-4000

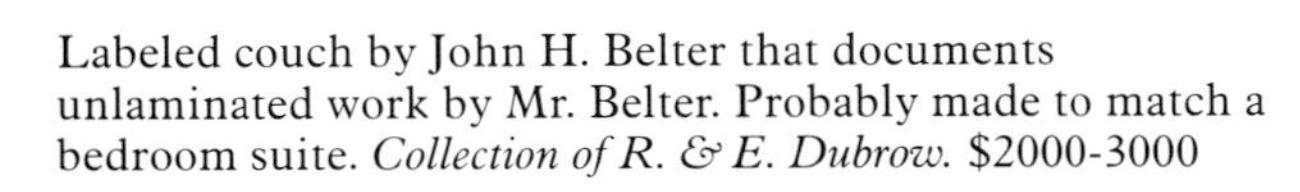

Labeled couch by John H. Belter that documents unlaminated work by Mr. Belter. Probably made to match a bedroom suite. *Collection of R. & E. Dubrow.* $2000-3000

Laminated rosewood John H. Belter couch with carved portrait bust of T. Jefferson, G. Washington and B. Franklin. *Photograph courtesy of R. & E. Dubrow. Collection of Gloria and Richard Manney.* $6000-8000

"Fountain Elms" pattern John H. Belter love seat. *Photograph courtesy of Munson - Williams - Proctor Institute.* $25,000-35,000

Pierced, laminated rosewood sofa attributed to John H. Belter in the "Tutthill King" pattern. *Photograph courtesy of R. & E. Dubrow.* $30,000-40,000

"Cornucopia" pattern John H. Belter love seat. Gift of Mr. and Mrs. Carl Vietor. *Photograph Museum of City of New York.* $50,000+

One of the most ornate examples of the laminated parlor furniture of John Henry Belter. Rosewood exterior layer. Center cresting is 28 inches high. *Collection of the Victoria and Albert Museum, London, England. Photograph courtesy of R. & E. Dubrow.* $50,000+

John H. Belter laminated, pierced sofa in the "Cornucopia" pattern. *Photograph courtesy of The Service collection.* $50,000+

Multiform card table by Charles A. Boudoine. The pair can be locked together to form a center table or separated to form a pair of console tables. Opened up, each one was a card table. *Photograph courtesy of the Munson-Williams-Proctor Institute.* $4000-6000

Multiform tables of rosewood by Charles A. Boudoine. These tables are a pair of card tables or can be hooked together to form a center table. *Photograph courtesy of R. & E. Dubrow. Private Collection.* $4000-6000

C. A. Baudoine
June 7. 1852
Furniture
$512.50
Paid by A. Munson

Detail of a bill from Charles A. Boudoine to James Watson Williams for parlor furniture, paid by A. Munson. *Photograph courtesy of the Munson-Williams-Proctor Institute. Fountain Elms Papers.*

New York May 26th 1852
Mr. J. Watson Williams
Bot of C A Baudoine
335 Broadway

1 Suit Rosewood Furniture in
Green Tapestry Viz
2 Tete a Tetes 4 Chairs & 2 Fauteuils } 340.
1 Rosewood Multiform Table 160.
Boxing 5 Boxes $2.50 12.50
$512.50

New York June 7th 1852
J W Williams Esq
D Sir
Above you have
Bill Furniture purchased 26th ulto
(amt $512.50) for which I have this day
drawn on you at sight
Very Respy Yours
C A Baudoine
pr B A Adams

Bill dated May 26, 1852 for furniture. Table in the next photo is covered by this bill. *Munson-Williams-Proctor Institute. Fountain Elms Paper.*

Charles A. Boudoine work table, circa 1846. *Photograph courtesy of the Munson-Williams-Proctor Institute. Proctor Collection.* $1500-2500

John Henry Belter console table. *Collection of Gloria and Richard Manney. Photograph courtesy of R. & E. Dubrow.*

Rare round Belter side/lamp table. *Photograph courtesy of Service Collection.* $20,000-30,000

Rococo revival laminated rosewood round lamp table. Maker unknown. *Gallier House. Photograph courtesy of R. & E. Dubrow.* $10,000-15,000

Labeled round Belter table. *Photograph courtesy of the Museum of City of New York - Gift of Mr. and Mrs. Carl Vietor.* $50,000+

J. & J. Meeks console table. *Photograph courtesy of R. & E. Dubrow.*

"Henry Ford" pattern turtle top table attributed to J. & J. Meeks. *Photograph courtesy of R. & E. Dubrow.* $15,000-20,000

Table attributed to John H. Belter. *Photograph courtesy of the White House Collection, Presidential Fund.* $50,000+

Rococo, pierced, carved 3-legged round table by a New York maker. *Photograph courtesy of the Metropolitan Museum of Art.* $15,000-25,000

Center table attributed to J. & J. Meeks. *Photograph courtesy of R. & E. Dubrow.* $10,000-15,000

Turtle top center table. Laminated Rosewood. Attributed to J. and J. Meeks. $15,000-20,000

Turtle top "Rosalie" pattern table with four carved dolphins. Collection of Mr. and Mrs. Donald Hurst. *Photograph courtesy of R. & E. Dubrow.* $20,000-25,000

Turtle top center table. *Photograph courtesy of Service Collection.* $35,000-45,000

Turtle top center table attributed to J.H. Belter. *Photograph courtesy of Mr. and Mrs. W. Sykora.* $35,000-45,000

Turtle top center table with portrait busts by John H. Belter. *Private collection. Photograph courtesy of R. & E. Dubrow.* $40,000-50,000

Side view of table showing cartouches.

Turtle top center table with rosewood top by John H. Belter. *Photograph courtesy of Service Collection.* $30,000-40,000

Turtle top center table by John H. Belter. *Photograph courtesy of the Newark Museum.* $50,000+

Partial label of table.

John H. Belter rosewood turtle top table in the "Rosalie" pattern. Note the dolphins and hanging grapes on each leg. *Photograph courtesy of The Service collection.* $20,000-25,000

Rosewood library table with inset marble possibly by Alexander Roux in New York. *Photograph courtesy of Richard & Eileen Dubrow.* $15,000-20,000

Laminated, rosewood table attributed to John H. Belter. *Photograph courtesy of the Munson-William Proctor Institute.* $4000-6000

Rosewood center table attributed to J. & J. Meeks. *Photograph courtesy of Morton's Auction Gallery.* $4000-6000

John Henry Belter round table of unusual size. Descended in the Gene Tierney family. Gloria and Richard Manney gift to the Metropolitan Museum of Art. *Photograph courtesy of Sotheby Parke Bernet.* $50,000+

Detail of pierced laminated table.

Wash stand attributed to Prudence Mallard. Gallier House. $300-500

Night stand attributed to Prudence Mallard. *Photograph courtesy of the Louisiana State Museum.* $800-1200

Carte de Visite by Broadbent & Company, Philadelphia.

Above Left
Dressing table attributed to Prudence Mallard. Gallier House. *Photograph courtesy of R. & E. Dubrow.* $4000-6000

Above Right
Dressing table attributed to Prudence Mallard. *Photograph courtesy of Frank Fasullo.* $5000-7000

Left
Labeled ladies' writing desk by Charles A. Boudoine, see page 93. *Photograph courtesy of the Museum of Fine Arts, Boston. Gift of William W. Banks Foundation in memory of Laurie Crechton.* $5000-7000

Opposite Page
Dressing table attributed to Prudence Mallard. *Photograph courtesy of the Louisiana State Museum.* $4000-6000

Above Left
Rosewood cabinet desk by John Jelliff, circa 1850-60. *Photograph courtesy of The Newark Museum.* $7000-9000

Above Right
Walnut and Burl drop lid desk by Brunner and Moore. *Photograph courtesy of Sotheby Parke Bernet.* $1500-2000

Right
Wash stand attributed to Prudence Mallard. *Photograph courtesy of the Louisiana State Museum.* $1000-1500

Opposite Page
Rosewood and walnut etagere bearing the stencil of Julius Dessoir, New York City, circa 1851-56. *Photograph courtesy of the Cooper Hewitt Museum. The Smithsonian Institution's National Museum of Design.* $10,000-15,000

Rosewood rococo dressing table. *Photograph courtesy of The Service Collection.* $8000-12,000

Rosewood fall front secretary attributed to Thomas Brooks of Brooklyn, New York. *Photograph courtesy of The Service Collection.* $8000-12,000

John H. Belter closed carved Rosewood etager. This piece is of exceptionally small proportions. *Photograph courtesy of The Service Collection.* $15,000-20,000

Rosewood etagere, probably by Daniel Pabst. *Photograph courtesy of R. & E. Dubrow.* $20,000-25,000

Laminated, pierced, rosewood etagere, 9 1/2 feet tall. Attributed to J. & J. Meeks. *Photograph courtesy of R. & E. Dubrow.* $20,000-25,000

Console/etagere by John H. Belter. *Photograph courtesy of the New York State Historical Society.* $50,000+

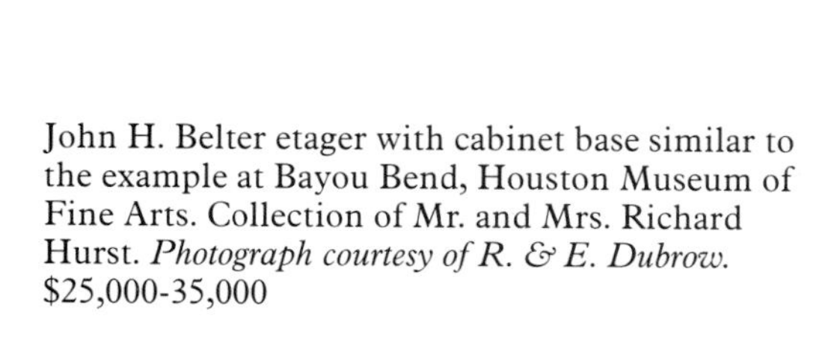

John H. Belter etager with cabinet base similar to the example at Bayou Bend, Houston Museum of Fine Arts. Collection of Mr. and Mrs. Richard Hurst. *Photograph courtesy of R. & E. Dubrow.* $25,000-35,000

Laminated, rosewood etagere in the "Rosalie" pattern by John H. Belter, circa 1855. *Photograph courtesy of The Service Collection.* $20,000-25,000

Details of John H. Belter "Rosalie" pattern etagere. *Photograph courtesy of The Service Collection.*

Opposite Page
John H. Belter etagere of laminated rosewood. *Photograph courtesy of Service Collection.* $35,000-45,000

Above
Detail of top crest with cupids & birds.

Right
Detail of cupid and bird.

Details of John H. Belter etagere. *Photograph courtesy of The Service Collection.*

Dolphin supports detailed.

Cupid at base with butterfly.

Armoir attributed to Prudence Mallard.
Photograph courtesy of Frank Fasullo.
$4000-5000

Two armoirs attributed to Prudence Mallard at Gallier House, New Orleans, Louisiana. *Photographs courtesy of R. & E. Dubrow.* $1500-2500 ea.

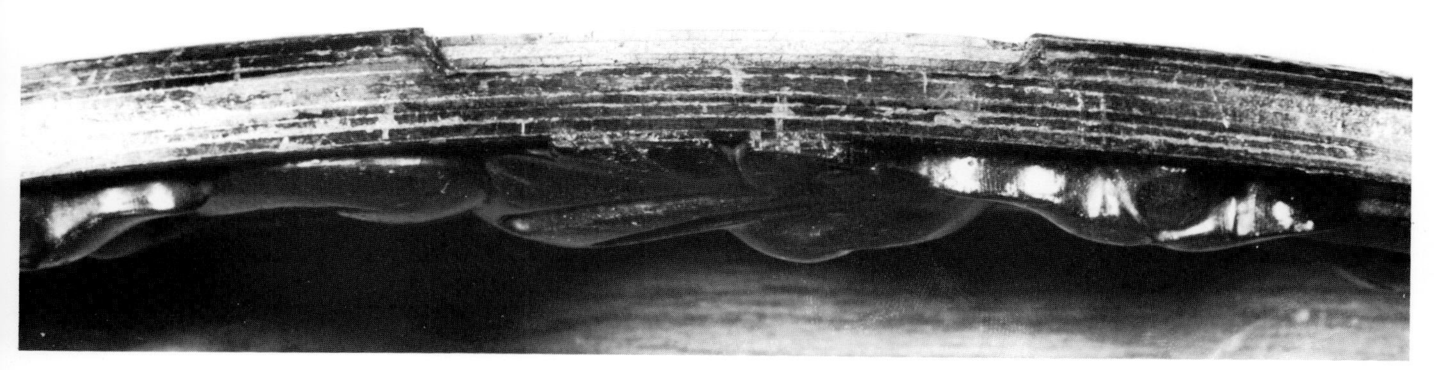

Opposite Page
John Henry Belter Rosewood dresser with serpentine front and sides and laminated drawers. Collection of R. & E. Dubrow. *Photograph courtesy of Edward J. Stanek and Douglas K. True.* $25,000-35,000

Above
Detail of top drawer and drawer insert from a Belter dresser. *Dresser not pictured.*

Center
Detail of laminations of dresser drawer. *Dresser not pictured.*

Right
Detail of impressed brand on Belter dresser. *Dresser not pictured.*

John Henry Belter Rosewood dresser.
Photograph courtesy of the Brooklyn Museum.
$50,000+

Rosewood dresser possibly by Mitchells and Rammelsburg.
Photograph courtesy of Service Collection. $4000-6000

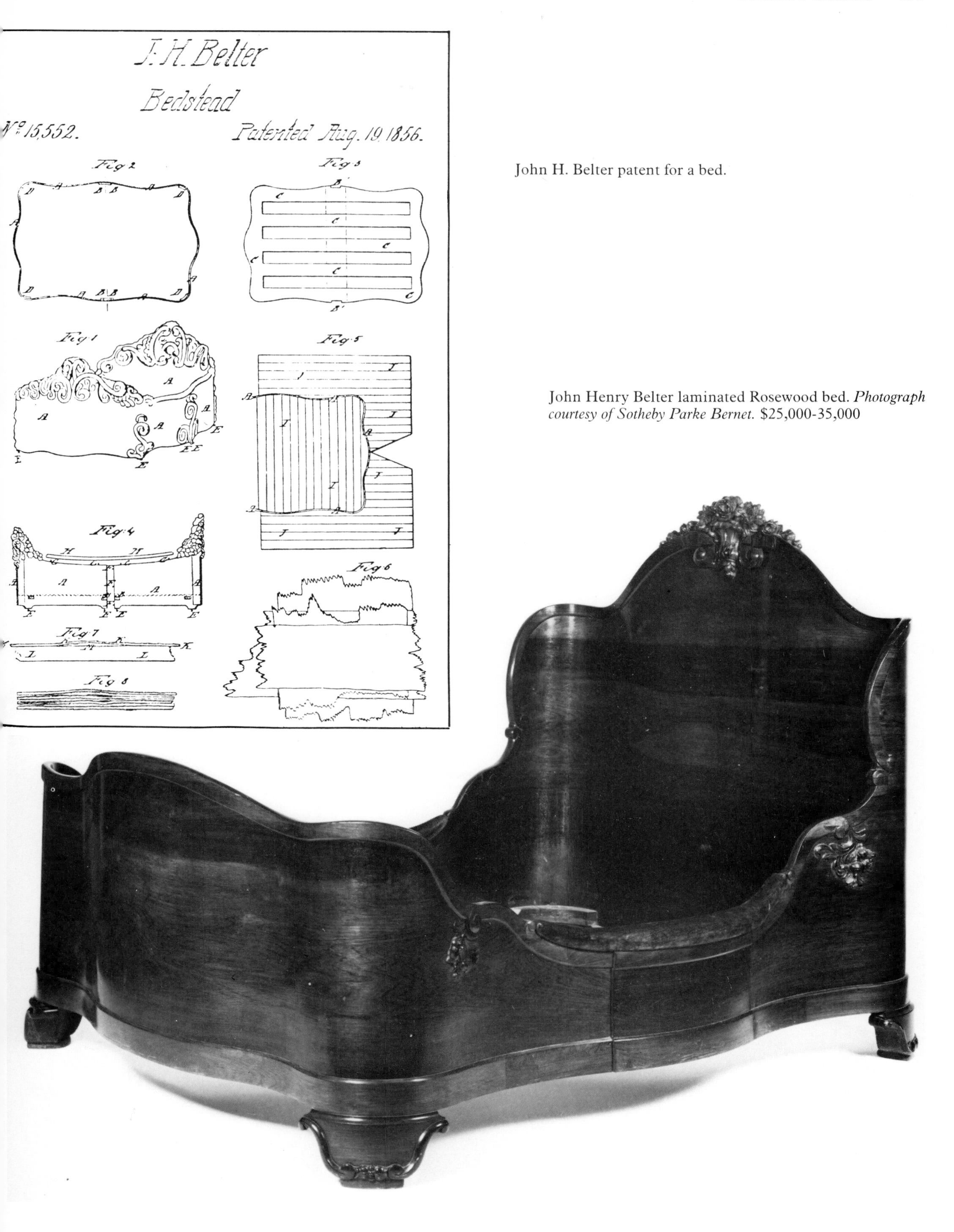

John H. Belter patent for a bed.

John Henry Belter laminated Rosewood bed. *Photograph courtesy of Sotheby Parke Bernet.* $25,000-35,000

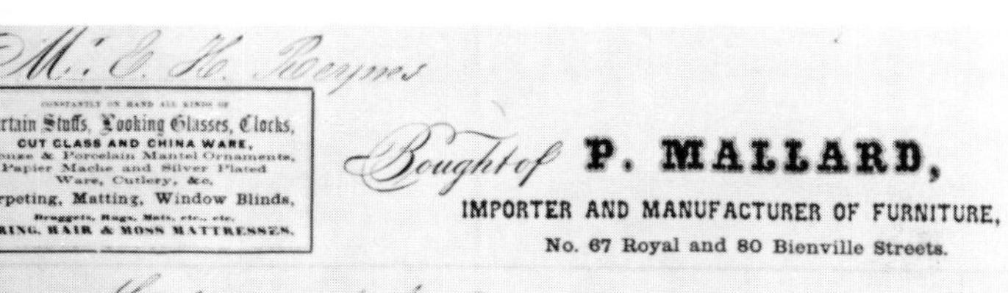
Bought of P. MALLARD,
IMPORTER AND MANUFACTURER OF FURNITURE,
No. 67 Royal and 80 Bienville Streets.

Prudence Mallard bill dated 1861. Note: Mallard was an importer and manufacturer of furniture.

Half-tester bed attributed to Prudence Mallard. Gallier House. *Photograph courtesy of R. & E. Dubrow.*

Opposite Page
Half-tester bed attributed to Prudence Mallard. *Photograph courtesy of the Louisiana State Museum.* $12,000-15,000

John Henry Belter bed. Carvings of cupids, butterflies and flowers. *Collection of Gloria and Richard Manney. Photograph courtesy of R. & E. Dubrow.* $50,000+

Impressed brand on side of John H. Belter bed, see page 155. *Photograph courtesy of Sotheby Parke Bernet.*

Above
Headboard of bed.

Center
Side rails of bed with lion carving.

Footboard of bed.

John Henry Belter Rosewood bed.
Photograph courtesy of the Brooklyn Museum. $50,000+

Rosewood headboard in the Rococo Style possibly by Mitchells and Rommelsberg.
Photograph courtesy of The Service Collection. $8000-12,000

Elizabethan Furniture

Elizabethan revival or cottage furniture, 1850-70, was mass produced, inexpensive furniture made of a variety of soft woods that when finished were painted and then often stenciled. The pieces were characterized by spiral or spool turned legs and stiles and referred back to Charles II and 17th century Flemish work. "Jenny Lind" furniture falls into this classification.

Alexander Roux dining room suite made in black walnut. Server and erving table have paper labels. *Photograph courtesy of Service Collection.*

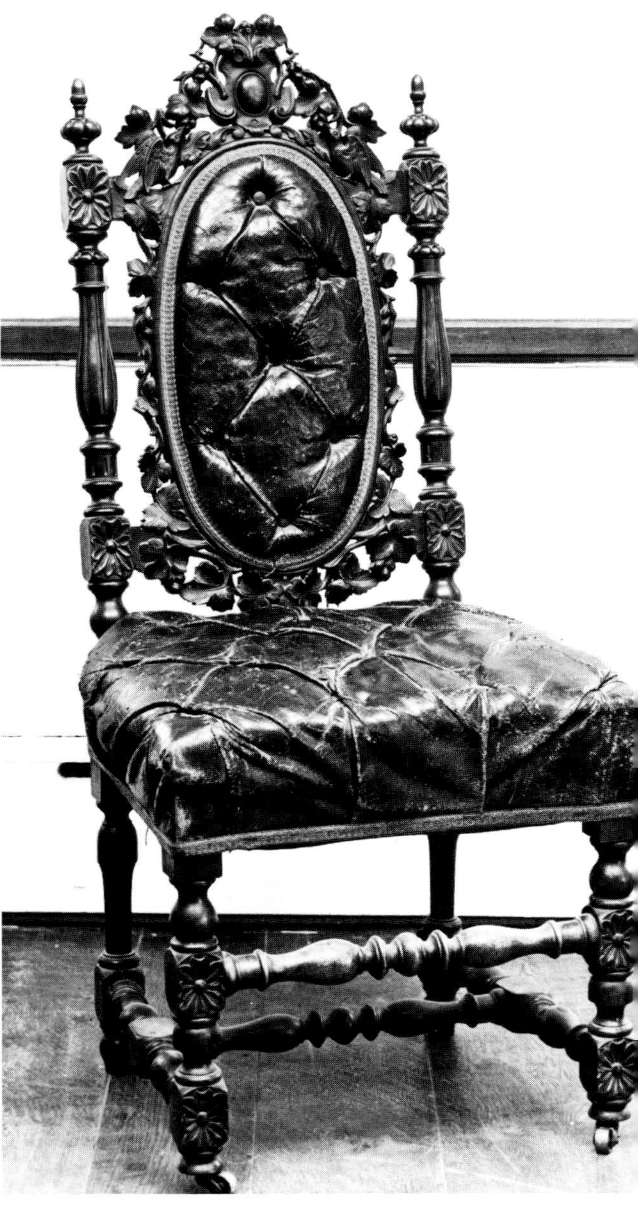

Above Left
Detail of side chair from the Alexander Roux suite. *Photograph courtesy of the Service Collection.*

Above Right
Dining chair from the Alexander Roux suite. *Photograph courtesy of the Service Collection.* $1000-1500

Arm chair from the Alexander Roux suite. *Photograph courtesy of R. & E. Dubrow.* $1500-2000

Interior views of unidentified home. *Photographs courtesy of Louisiana State University Library.*

Heywood Brothers & Company office arm chair. *Photograph courtesy of the Indianapolis Museum of Art. Gift of Dr. Truman S. Grayson.* $100-200

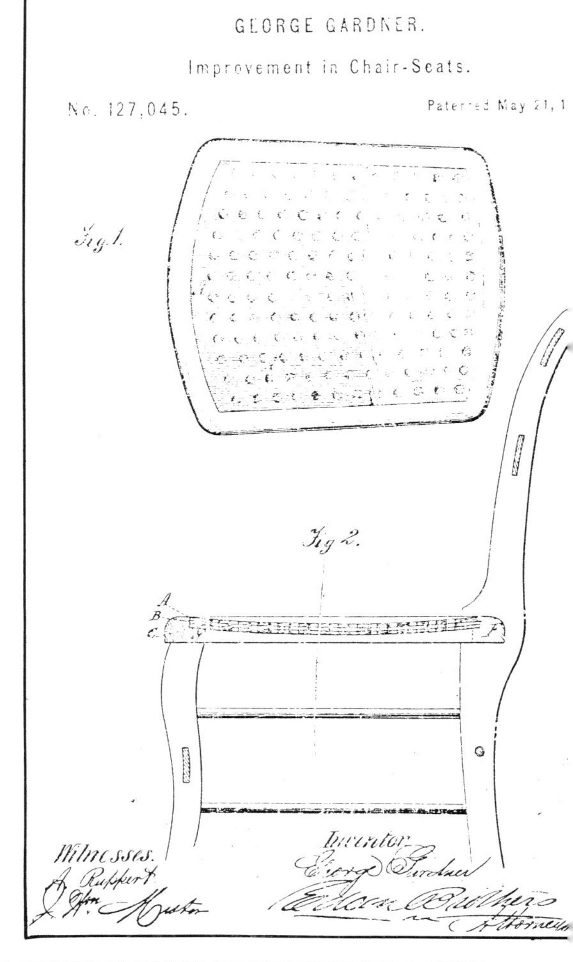

Rocking chair. $100-200

Side chair. $100-200

Painted cottage bedroom suite probably from the Hennesey firm in Boston. This set was painted by a family member, A.B. Lawrence, in 1846. *Photograph courtesy of E. & C. Stone.* $400-600

Table. $200-300

Night stand. $300-500

Alexander Roux dining table in the Elizabethan style. Wood is black walnut. *The Service Collection. Photograph courtesy of R. & E. Dubrow.* $5000-7000

Detail of table.

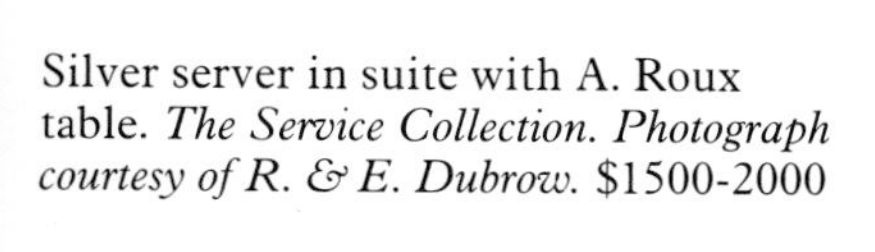

Silver server in suite with A. Roux table. *The Service Collection. Photograph courtesy of R. & E. Dubrow.* $1500-2000

Detail of carving on A. Roux table. *The Service Collection. Photograph courtesy of R. & E. Dubrow.*

A. Roux label on underside of serving table. *The Service Collection. Photograph courtesy of R. & E. Dubrow.*

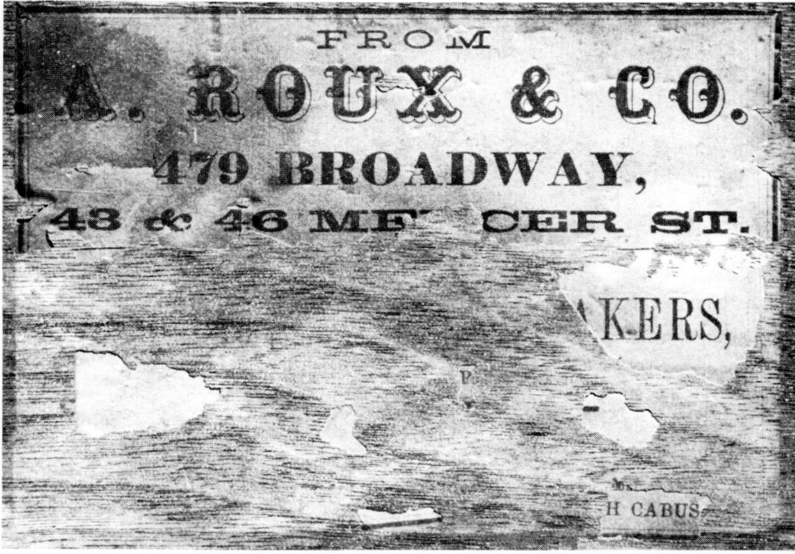

Side board in suite with A. Roux table. *The Service Collection. Photograph courtesy of R. & E. Dubrow.* $8000-12,000

A. Roux label affixed to underside of side board. *The Service Collection. Photograph of R. & E. Dubrow.*

Chest of drawers by Hart, Ware & Company. *Photograph courtesy of the Philadelphia Museum of Art.* $800-1200

"Elizabethan" style cottage bureau, circa 1850. *Photograph courtesy of Sotheby Parke Bernet.* $1000-1500

Elizabethan style spool bed.
$200-300

Bureau and bed from the painted cottage bedroom suite probably from the Hennesey firm in Boston. The set was painted by A.B. Lawrence in 1846. *Photograph courtesy of E. & C. Stone.* $600-800

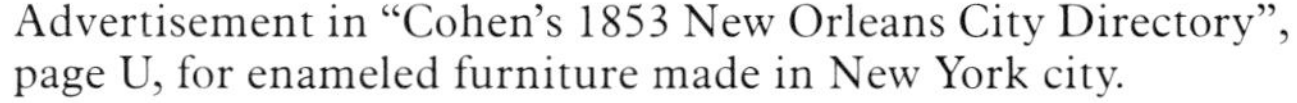

Advertisement in "Cohen's 1853 New Orleans City Directory", page U, for enameled furniture made in New York city.

WARREN WARD

Wholesale and Retail Manufacturer of

ENAMELED FURNITURE,

NO. 144 GRAND STREET, NEW YORK.

MR. WARD gives his whole attention to the manufacturing; and from using the best materials he feels assured that he offers better and cheaper Goods than can be found elsewhere, if quality and prices are compared.

Suits finished to match from $25 to $250 pr Suit

Consisting of *Dressing Bureau with Glass, Bedstead, Washstand, Commode, Toilet Table, Towel Stand, Nurse Rocker and Four Chairs.*

NO. 144 GRAND STREET,

One Block east of Broadway, New York.

Renaissance Furniture

American Renaissance furniture made between 1860 and 1875 was characterized by massive form, deeply carved ornaments, portrait medallions and square form. The architectural forms were used decoratively rather than structurally. The rooms became richer in detail losing the sense of stylistic isolation that was present in earlier centuries. Also included in this category are the Egyptian influenced pieces since they are merely variants of Renaissance with their applied Egyptian inspired ornaments of palms, beetles and sphinxes.

Music room in the residence of Judge Augustus Macon, Canyon City, Colorado, circa 1890. *Photograph courtesy of the Colorado Historical Society.*

Room settings in the Lockwood Mathews Mansion.

Parlor in the residence of Judge Augustus Macon, Canyon City, Colorado, circa 1890. *Photograph courtesy of the Colorado Historical Society.*

Room setting in Baltimore. *Photograph courtesy of R. & E. Dubrow.*

Room setting in Baltimore. Note the wire seated Hunzinger patent rocker on the right.

Patent "Fancy chairs" by George Hunzinger. The chair on the left has a patent wire seat. *Photograph courtesy of R. & E. Dubrow.* $300-500 ea.

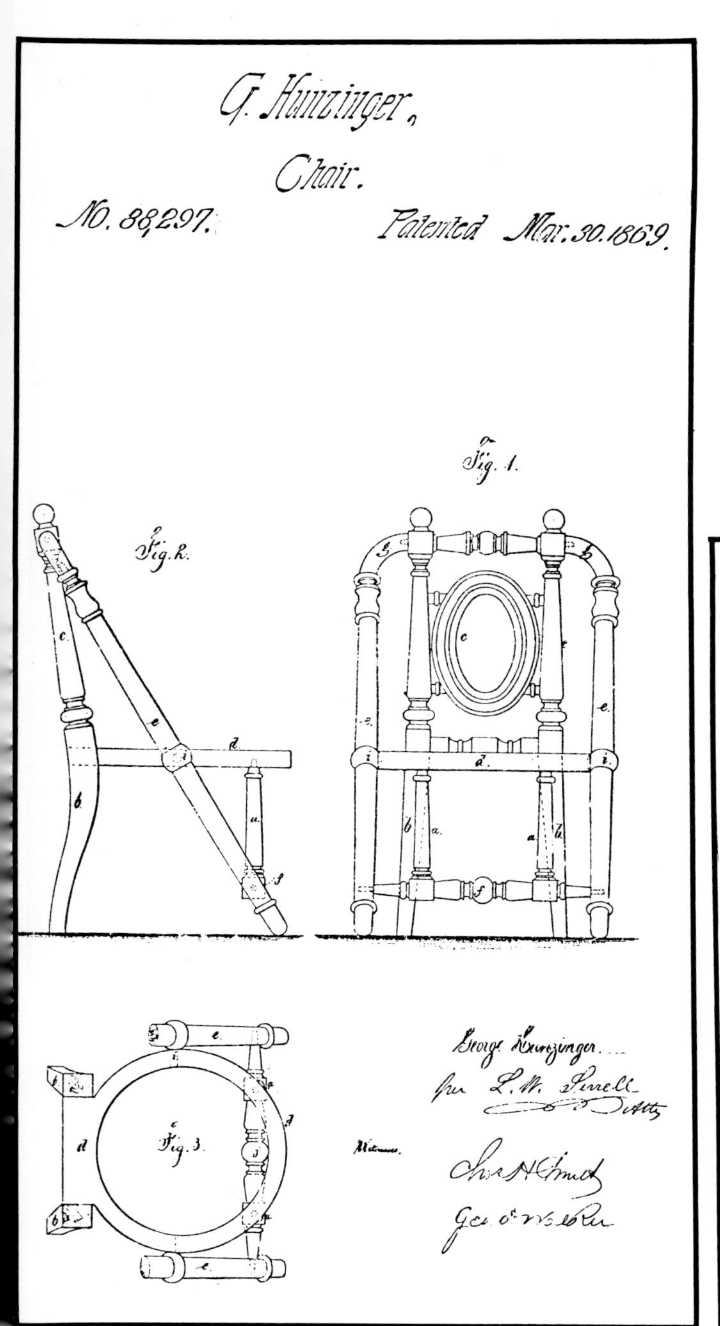
G. Hunzinger,
Chair.
No. 88,297.
Patented Mar. 30. 1869.
Fig. 1.
Fig. 2.
Fig. 3.

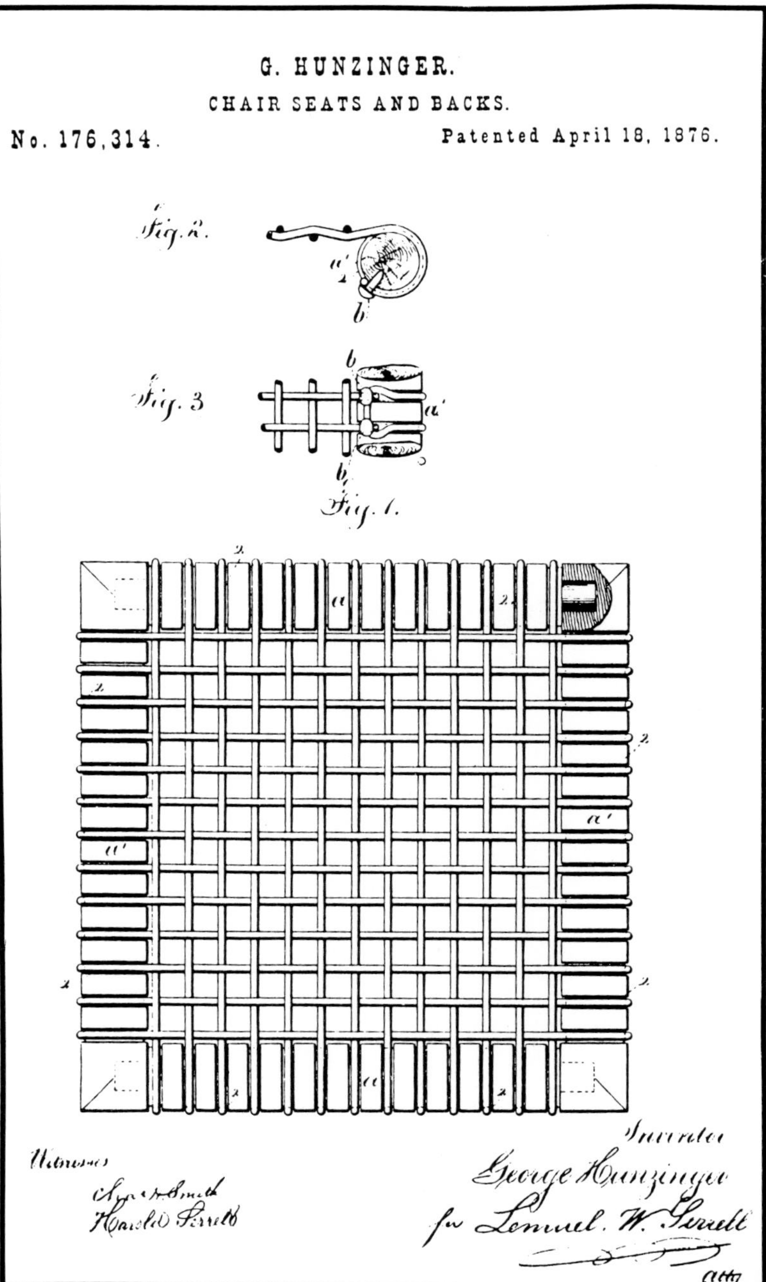
G. HUNZINGER.
CHAIR SEATS AND BACKS.
No. 176,314.
Patented April 18, 1876.
Fig. 2.
Fig. 3
Fig. 1.

George Hunzinger patented duplex spring rocker. *Photograph courtesy of Sotheby Parke Bernet.* L-R: $800-1000, $1500-2000

George Hunzinger patent folding chairs. *Photograph courtesy of Sotheby Parke Bernet.* 300-500 ea.

American Renaissance Revival ebonized and gilt incised Gentleman's arm chair, circa 1865, possibly Herter Bros. *Photograph courtesy of Sotheby's L.A.* $5000-7000

Renaissance Revival side chair by unknown maker bearing many similarities to documented work by George Hunzinger. *Photograph courtesy of The Service Collection.* $400-500

Folding chair bearing the label of E.W. Vaill, Worcester, Massachusetts, 1868. *Photograph courtesy of the Indianapolis Museum of Art.* $200-300

Renaissance Revival walnut Lady's arm chair by an unknown maker. *Photograph courtesy of Sotheby's L.A.* $800-1200

Walnut arm chair by John Jelliff, circa 1850. *Photograph courtesy of The Newark Museum.* $2000-3000

Set of unidentified Renaissance Revival furniture circa 1875 probably made in Philadelphia. *Photograph courtesy of the Library Company of Philadelphia.* Top row: $300-500 ea. Bottom, L-R: $400-600, $500-700, $300-500

Renaissance Revival walnut side chair by an unknown maker. *Photograph courtesy of Sotheby's L.A.* $800-1200

Set of unidentified Renaissance Revival furniture circa 1875 probably made in Philadelphia. *Photograph courtesy of the Library Company of Philadelphia.* Top row: $300-500 ea. Bottom, L-R: $400-600, $500-700, $300-500

Above
Library step chair - Kimbel & Cabus design book. *Photographs courtesy of the Smithsonian Institution.* $1000-1500

Renaissance Revival ebonized and gilt incised maple sofa, circa 1865, possibly Herter Brothers. *Photograph courtesy of Sotheby's L.A.* $10,000-15,000

George Hunzinger parlor set, note hoofed feet. *Photograph courtesy of Sotheby Parke Bernet.* $8000-12,000

Rosewood sofa with mother-of-pearl medallion by John Jelliff, circa 1860. *Photograph courtesy of The Newark Museum.* $3000-5000

Upholstered Kimbel & Cabus couch from their design book. *Photograph courtesy of the Smithsonian Institution.* $2000-3000

Kimbel & Cabus settee. *Photograph courtesy of the Smithsonian Institution.* $2000-3000

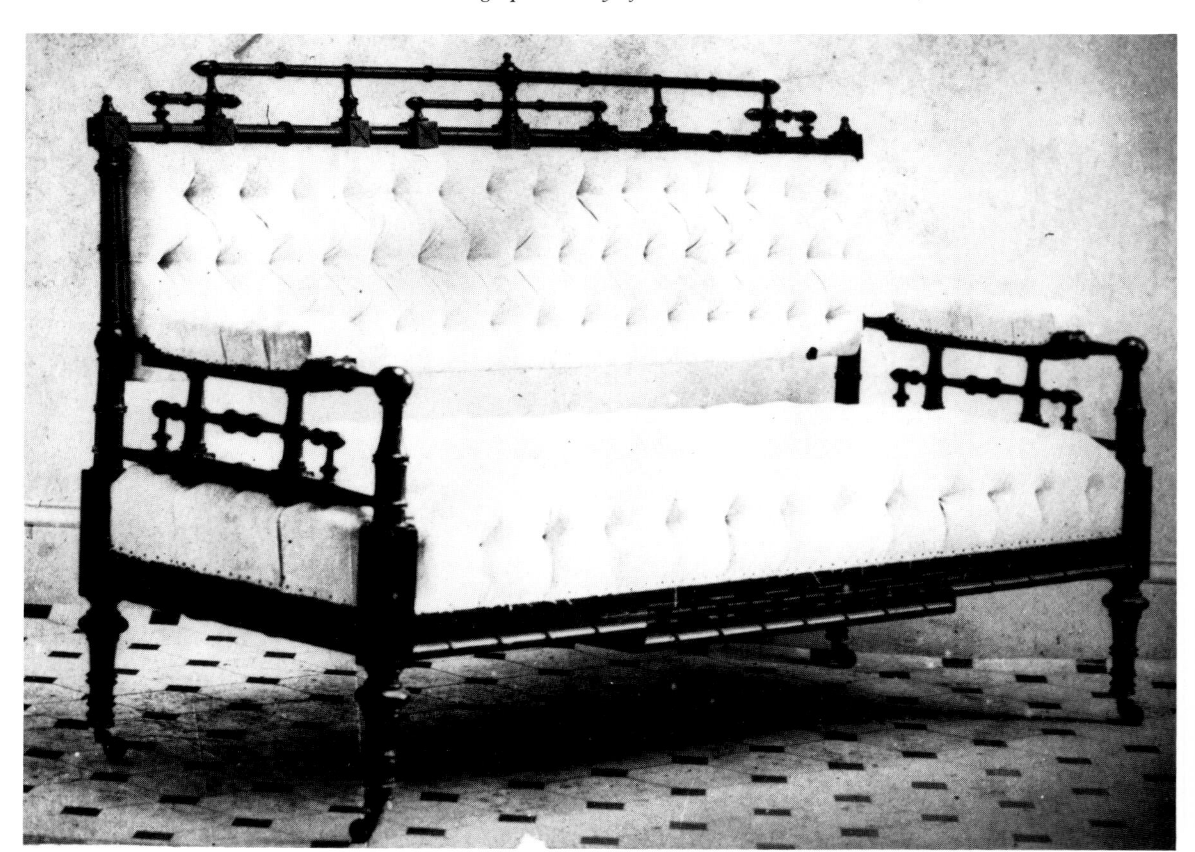

Card table attributed to Alexander Roux. *Photograph courtesy of the Brooklyn Museum, H. Randolph Lever Fund.* $3000-5000

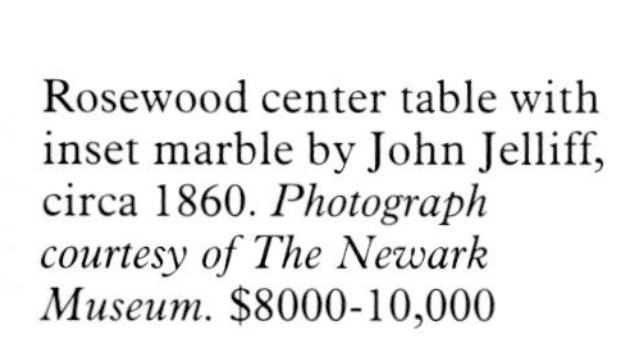

Rosewood center table with inset marble by John Jelliff, circa 1860. *Photograph courtesy of The Newark Museum.* $8000-10,000

Side or lamp table with inlaid top by Berkey and Gay. *Photograph courtesy of the Grand Rapids Public Museum.* $2000-3000

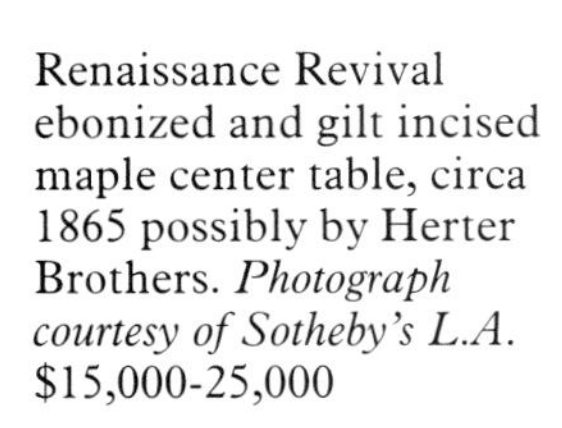

Renaissance Revival ebonized and gilt incised maple center table, circa 1865 possibly by Herter Brothers. *Photograph courtesy of Sotheby's L.A.* $15,000-25,000

Kimel & Cabus book rack from their design book. *Photograph courtesy of the Smithsonian Institution.* $10,000-15,000

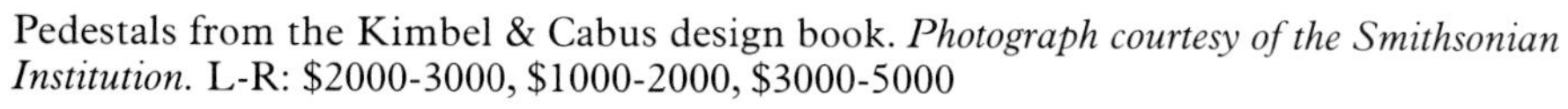

Pedestals from the Kimbel & Cabus design book. *Photograph courtesy of the Smithsonian Institution.* L-R: $2000-3000, $1000-2000, $3000-5000

Tag from the Wooton desk made for his distributor F. & J. Smith in Glasgow, Scotland, patented in 1875 there rather than 1874 in America.

U.S. Patent Office display at the Philadelphia Centennial in 1876. Note the Wooton Desk in center on platform.

Wooton "Extra Grade" double pier rotary desk, the "Lawyers Own". *Photography courtesy of R. & E. Dubrow.* L-R: $3000-5000, $300-500

Stereopticon cards showing the building at 32 South Holiday Street, Baltimore, Maryland [left] where General Shipley [right] used the Wooton desk in his office. *Photograph courtesy of R. & E. Dubrow.*

John D. Rockefeller's "Extra Grade" Wooton Patent Secretary. *Photograph courtesy of Sleepy Hollow Restorations, Philips Castle, Tarrytown, New York.* $15,000-20,000

Wooton Desk at Iolani Palace, Honolulu, Hawaii. *Photograph courtesy of the Honolulu Academy of Arts.* $12,000-20,000

Right
The first installation of the Smithsonian Institution 1976 Centennial display showing Wooton Desks lent by Richard and Eileen Dubrow. "Superior Grade" patent secretary, "Lawyers Own" double pier rotary desk, and "Extra Grade" patent secretary. $25,000-35,000

Below
A second installation of the Smithsonian Institution 1976 Centennial display showing Wooton Desks lent by Richard and Eileen Dubrow. Left to right: "Superior Grade" patent secretary, "Lawyers Own" double pier rotary desk, and "Extra Grade" patent secretary.

A third installation of the 1976 Smithsonian Institution display left to right: Ebonized "Superior Grade" prototype Secretary, "Extra Grade" Lawyers Own, only known model of Ladies Desk. $20,000-25,000

"Eastlake style" version of Standard Grade, Wooton Patent Secretary, with a double tier gallery - not shown in any catalogue. *Photograph courtesy of R. & E. Dubrow.*

Wooton Ladies patent secretary - only known model. *Photograph courtesy of R. & E. Dubrow.* $20,000-25,000

Joseph Moore Desk, "Extra Grade" model, closed view. Collection of Dr. and Mrs. J. Stichen. *Photograph courtesy of R. & E. Dubrow.* $6000-8000

Moore Desk, open view. *Photograph courtesy of R. & E. Dubrow.*

WM. S. WOOTON,
Of Richmond, Ind.
R. L. TALBOT,
Indianapolis.
WM. S. WOOTON & CO.,
MANUFACTURERS AND DEALERS IN
School, Office and Church
FURNITURE,
OFFICE, 115 East Washington St.,
INDIANAPOLIS, IND.
Send for Circular

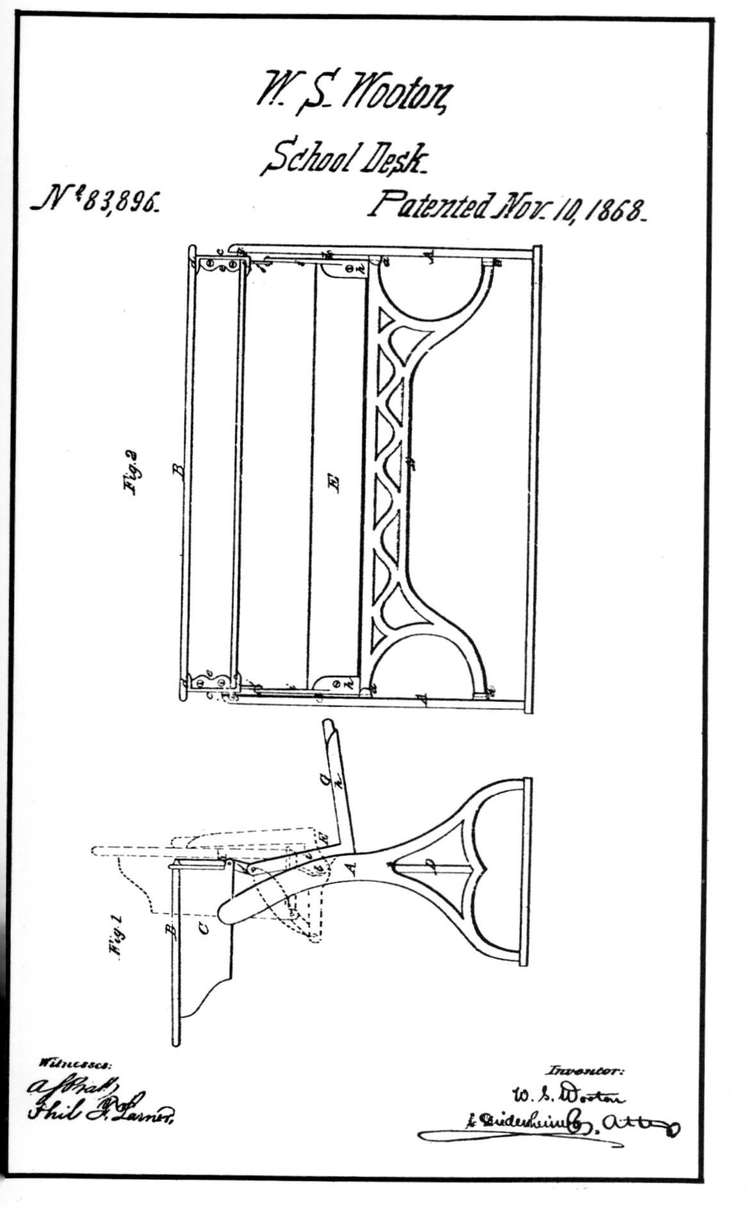
W. S. Wooton,
School Desk.
No. 83,896.
Patented Nov. 10, 1868.
Fig. 2
Fig. 1
Witnesses:
Inventor:

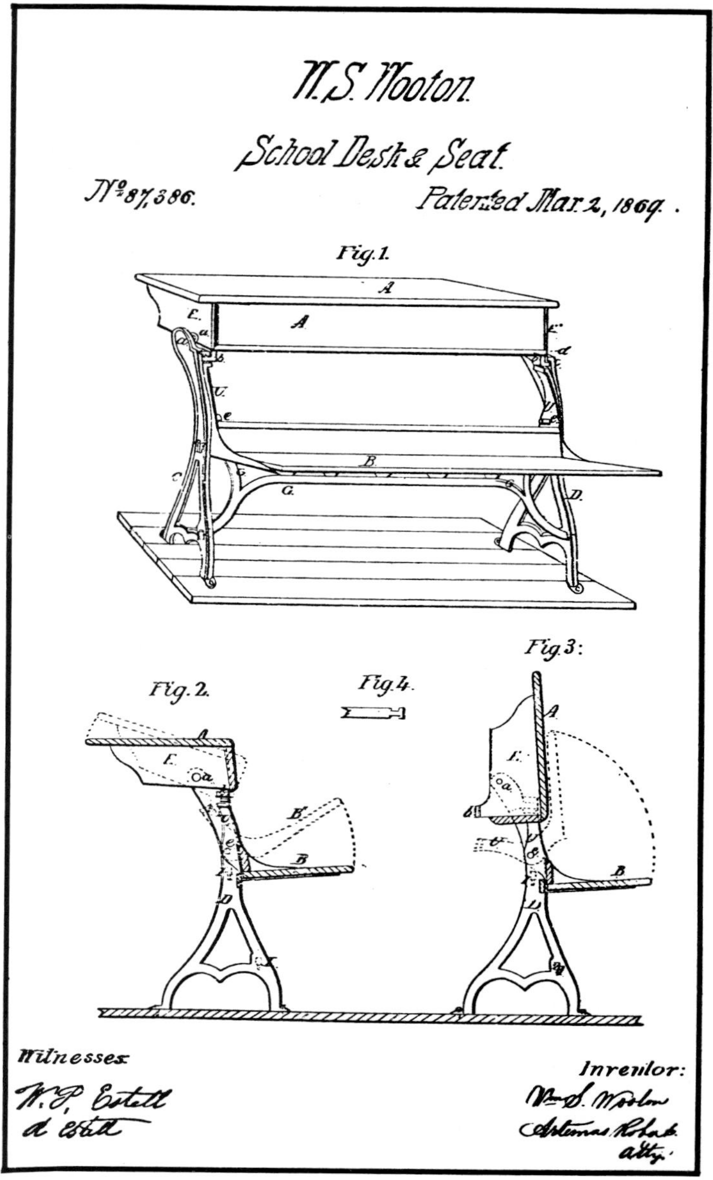
W. S. Wooton.
School Desk & Seat.
No. 87,386.
Patented Mar. 2, 1869.
Fig. 1.
Fig. 2.
Fig. 3.
Fig. 4.
Witnesses
W. P. Estell
Inventor:

"Superior Grade" Wooton Desk made for his distributor F. & J. Smith, 45 Gordon Street, Glasgow, Scotland. *Photograph courtesy of R. & E. Dubrow.* $8000-12,000

Same desk as above, note how plain and unadorned this model is. Supports for writing board are not slides. Desk has no mail slot. Plate on desk is marked "Wooton Desk Co. patented May 1, 1875" with the Glasgow address.

"Standard Grade" Wooton Desk at the San Bernadino County Museum. $8000-12,000

Dear fellow desk 6 March (1975)

I see from the "New York Times" that a society has been formed especially for us and I though you might like to know that you have a relative in Canada. The man who is writing this for me says that he has the Walters booklet. I am apparently a Standard model of the smallest size. I look identical to the Baird desk and to the catalogue illustrations. The man is too stupid to say what wood I'm made of but he does aver that I'm in excellent condition. I have all my interior fittings and file boxes and my hardware. Alas someone has handled me carelessly at some time and a section at the very bottom of one wing is missing as is one double caster. Someone has also drilled a small hole through my left wing and put a lock (which doesn't seem to be connected to anything) above my handle, both hole and hook being in the moulding at the top of the vertical part of my wings. Why did someone do that? My original lock and key are still with me and work perfectly.

Some of my hardware is just a little different from the photos in Walters, Fig 6. The escutcheons on my letter slot and name plaque are of a slightly different pattern, more "Rounded off" than squared and sharp-pointed-though my door handle is exactly like the photo. My plaque reads: Manufactured by the Wooton Desk Co. Indianapolis, Ind. Pat. Oct 6, 1974.

How did I get here? I've been in Montreal for a long time. The man is sure I was the property of his grandfather, who arrived here from Scotland in 1854 and died in 1910, so he may well have bought me new at birth. I've certainly lived in this building, which was constructed in 1913/15 for longer than the man can really recall. By some imperceptible process it seems I'm now the property of a family company of which the man says he is the president. So I'm a one-family desk! I am not looking for a new home and the man assures me that I'm positively not for sale, though I might go to a (preferably Canadian) museum. I thought you would like to hear from me anyway and to know that I feel fine and am happy. I hope this reaches you safely and in the approved fashion i.e. by being dropped into your letter slot and that it finds you in good health and trim. The man signs on my behalf.

Guy Drummond

Letter from a Wooton desk-owner's desk to a desk-owner-society's desk.

"Extra Grade" Wooton Patent Secretary. $15,000-20,000

Wooton double pier rotary "Cashiers desk" not shown in any catalogue. Drawing done by D.R. Clark, Indianapolis, Indiana for the Wooton Desk Company. *Photograph courtesy of R. & E. Dubrow.* $4000-6000

"Superior Grade" Wooton Patent secretary. *Photograph courtesy of R. & E. Dubrow.* $20,000-25,000

Open view "Superior Grade" Wooton Patent Secretary. *Photograph courtesy of R. & E. Dubrow.*

THE CELEBRATED WOOTON DESKS!

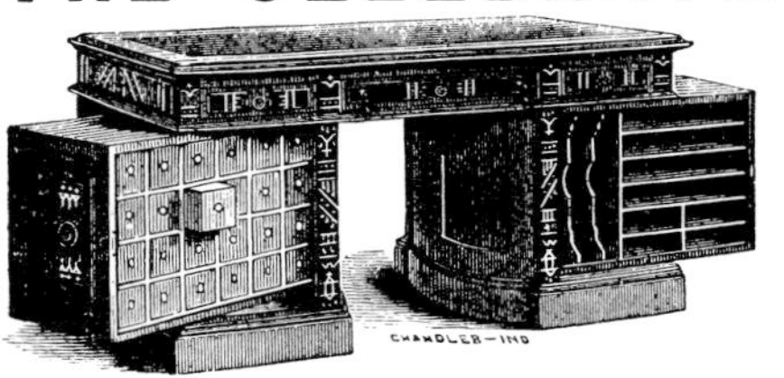

Solid Comfort Office Appliances.

EVERYBODY DELIGHTED WITH THEM.

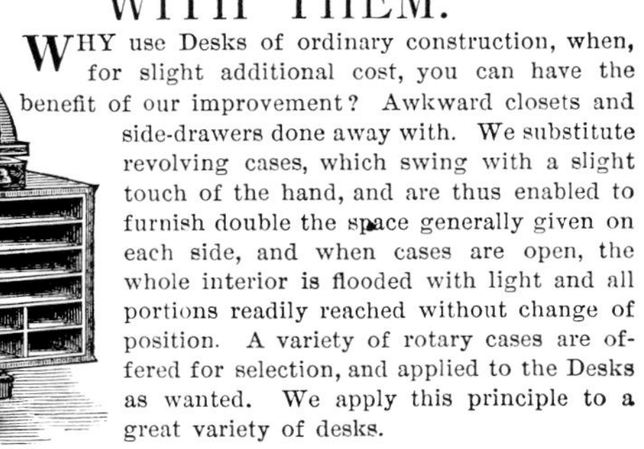

WHY use Desks of ordinary construction, when, for slight additional cost, you can have the benefit of our improvement? Awkward closets and side-drawers done away with. We substitute revolving cases, which swing with a slight touch of the hand, and are thus enabled to furnish double the space generally given on each side, and when cases are open, the whole interior is flooded with light and all portions readily reached without change of position. A variety of rotary cases are offered for selection, and applied to the Desks as wanted. We apply this principle to a great variety of desks.

For paticulars, address

THE WOOTON DESK M'F'G CO., Indianapolis, Ind., U. S. A.

131

Wooton "Extra Grade" double pier rotary desk - closed. Note variations in carving. *Photograph courtesy of R. & E. Dubrow.* $3000-4000

Wooton double pier rotary flat top desk. Not shown in any catalogue. *Photograph courtesy of R. & E. Dubrow.*

Wooton "Extra Grade" double pier rotary desk - open.

Renaissance revival bookcase/bureau by Thomas Brooks of Brooklyn. *Photograph courtesy of Sotheby Parke Bernet.* $15,000-20,000

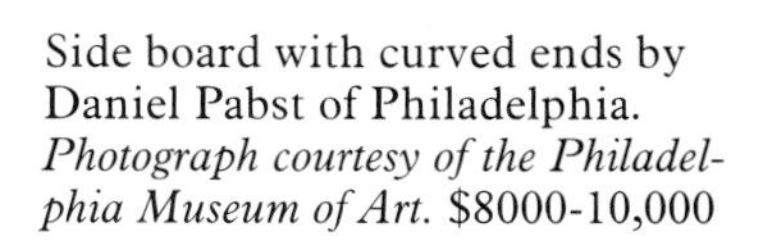

Side board with curved ends by Daniel Pabst of Philadelphia. *Photograph courtesy of the Philadelphia Museum of Art.* $8000-10,000

Curio cabinet, George C. Flint. *Photograph courtesy of the Metropolitan Museum of Art, Edgar J. Kaufman Charitable Foundation 1968.* $15,000-20,000

Drop front desk with what-not shelves from the Kimbel & Cabus design book. *Photograph courtesy of the Smithsonian Institution.* $10,000-15,000

Kimbel & Cabus etagere or what-not. *Photograph courtesy of the Smithsonian Institution.* L-R: $7000-10,000, $1000-1500.

Kimbel & Cabus what-not. *Photograph courtesy of the Smithsonian Institution.* L-R: $3000-5000, $4000-6000

T. Brooks dresser, Renaissance Revival styling. *Photograph courtesy of Sotheby Parke Bernet.* $5000-7000

Mitchells and Rammelberg dressing bureau, circa 1875, Cincinnati, Ohio. *Photograph courtesy of the Indianapolis Museum of Art. Gift of Mr. & Mrs. Robert Dooley in memory of Dr. & Mrs. Harrison C. Rice & Major & Mrs. Franklin Stevenson.* $1000-1500

Extremely ornate Renaissance revival dressing table. *Photograph courtesy of the Service Collection.* $8000-10,000

Rosewood bedstead by Alexander Roux. *Photograph courtesy of Sotheby Parke Bernet.* $2000-3000

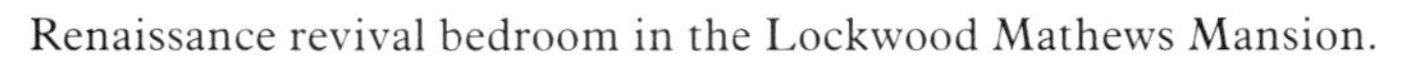

Renaissance revival bedroom in the Lockwood Mathews Mansion.

Above
Renaissance bedroom of Mrs. Marion Furness Ramsey. *Photograph courtesy of the Minnesota Historical Society.* $900-1100

Mitchells and Rammelsberg bedstead, circa 1875, Cincinnati, Ohio. *Photograph courtesy of the Indianapolis Museum of Art. Gift of Mr. & Mrs. Robert Dooley in memory of Dr. & Mrs. Harrison C. Rice & Major & Mrs. Franklin Stevenson.* $700-900

Bed by T. Brooks. *Photograph courtesy of Sotheby Parke Bernet.* $15,000-20,000

T. Brooks stencil. *Photograph courtesy of Sotheby Parke Bernet.*

Bedroom suite by Berkey and Gay. *Photograph courtesy of the Grand Rapids Public Museum.* $20,000-25,000

Below
Renaissance revival bedroom suite. *Photograph courtesy of Jay Anderson.* $12,000-15,000

Exceptional bedstead probably Mitchells and Rammelsberg. *Photograph courtesy Service Collection.*

Dresser and work stand en suite with bed. $20,000-30,000 (suite).

Hall mirror in the Renaissance style by Robert Renwick. *Photograph courtesy of Sotheby Parke Bernet.* $3000-5000

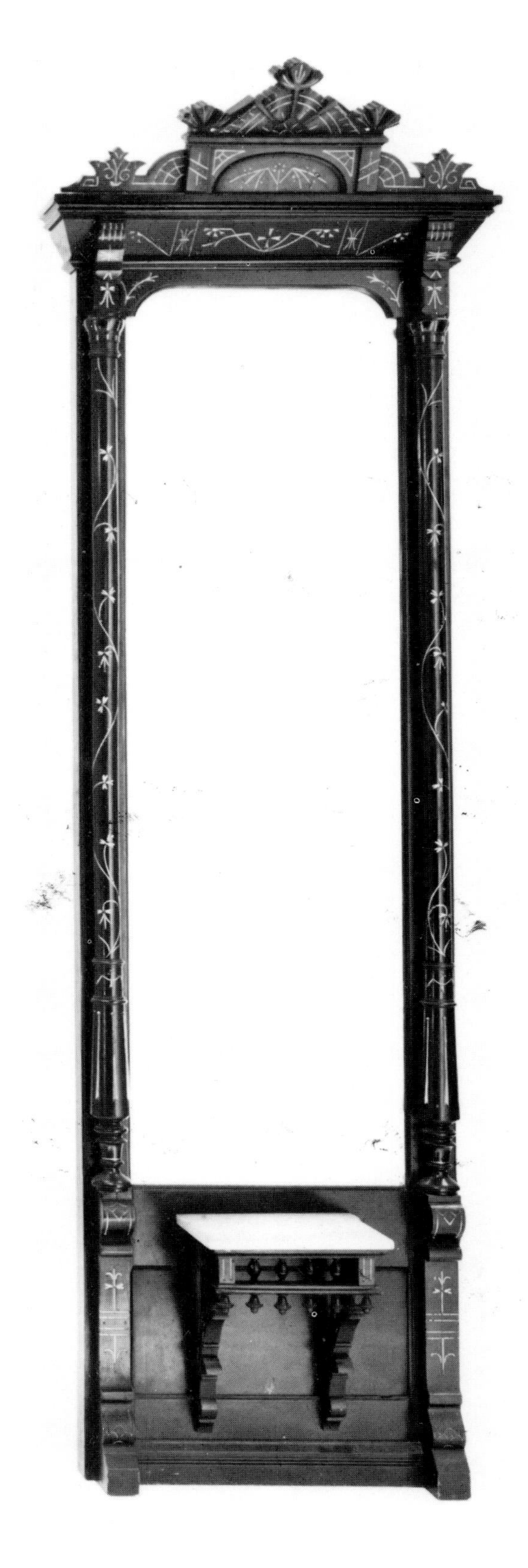

American Renaissance ebonized and walnut pier mirror, circa 1875. *Photograph courtesy of Sotheby's L.A.* $1200-1500

Renaissance Revival etagere, circa 1865. *Photograph courtesy of Sotheby Parke Bernet.*
$9000-11,000

Aesthetic Movement Fore-runners

The aesthetic movement in the United States shows its strongest influence between 1860 and 1890. Forerunners were firms like Herter Brothers, Pattier and Stymus and Kimbel and Cabus. The precepts were set by architects like Burger and Shaw and by designers like Morris. The furniture is distinguished by:

1.) The use of contrasting materials.
2.) Marquetry or other flat surface decoration (like painting)
3.) Rectilinear shapes.
4.) Sturdy construction.
5.) Some pieces were Anglo-Japanese influenced in the belief that Japanese art had the same simplicity and honest construction that these taskmakers liked in Medieval work.

Chairs by the firm of Pottier & Stymus. *Photographs courtesy of the Richardson Bates House.*

Pottier & Stymus arm chair made for the home of Auguste Pottier. *Photograph courtesy of the Museum of The City of New York.* $5000-7000

Side chair by Pottier & Stymus made for the home of Auguste Pottier. *Photograph courtesy of The City of New York.* $5000-7000

Side chair circa 1875 said to be part of a set that was awarded first prize at the Centennial Exhibition of 1876. *Photograph courtesy of the Museum of The City of New York.* $1000-1500

Side chair by Herter Brothers. *Photograph courtesy of the Philadelphia Museum of Art, Given by Mrs. William T. Carter.* $10,000-15,000

Walnut hall stand - Herter Brothers. *Photograph courtesy of Sotheby Parke Bernet.* $2000-3000

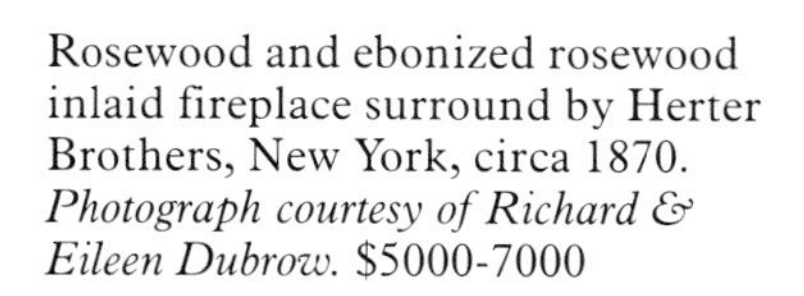

Rosewood and ebonized rosewood inlaid fireplace surround by Herter Brothers, New York, circa 1870. *Photograph courtesy of Richard & Eileen Dubrow.* $5000-7000

Louis XVI Furniture

Louis XVI revival seems to have been launched as early as 1850 by George Srobe for Empress Eugene. In these pieces, straight lines and smooth marquetry surfaces replace the curves and carving of Rococo. The pieces do not have cabriole legs but do seem to incorporate the classical revival sponsored by the Adams Brothers from the 1750s. Most American made pieces have oval backs, straight stiles, ormolu or porcelain mounts, and ebonized finishes. This style was favored by Leon Marcotte and well made by Thomas Brooks, the Sypher Firm, Herter Brothers, John Jelliff, and George Henkels.

Room setting in the Lockwood Mathews Mansion.

Couch and side chairs by Gotlieb Vollmer. *Photograph courtesy of the Smithsonian Institution.* $4000-6000 (suite).

Side chairs and stools by Gotlieb Vollmer. *Photograph courtesy of the Smithsonian Institution.* $1800-2200 (all).

Arm chairs by Gottlieb Vollmer. *Photographs courtesy of the Philadelphia Museum of Art.* Top, $1000-1500; Bottom, $800-1200.

Table and sofa by Leon Marcotte. *Photograph courtesy of the Metropolitan Museum of Art.* Top, $4000-6000; Bottom, $2000-3000

Inlaid cabinet by Gottlieb Vollmer, Philadelphia, Pennsylvania, circa 1870. *Photograph courtesy of Private collection.* $2000-2500

Stenciled and painted pine armoire attributed to Leon Marcotte, circa 1865. *Photograph courtesy of Sotheby's L.A.*

Neo Grec Furniture

Neo Grec is the term used to classify the square, geometric heavier furniture of this period. While the name is not really the proper one for want of a better one we will use it for the pieces of heavy turned legs, classical entablatures of bronze and porcelain, incised lines and contrasting light and dark woods. Some of the pieces also reflect curule and Klismos styling.

Suite of furniture manufactured by the M. & H. Schrenkeisen Manufacturing Company of New York, New York.

Turkish patent rocking chairs made by the M. & H. Schrenkeisen Manufacturing Company of New York.

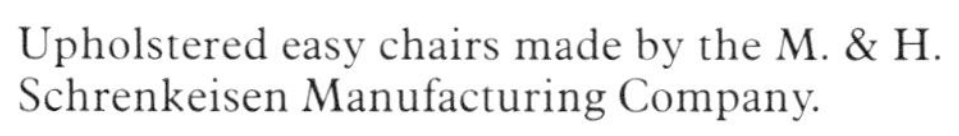

Upholstered easy chairs made by the M. & H. Schrenkeisen Manufacturing Company.

Parlor suite made by the M. & H. Schrenkeisen Manufacturing Company.

Above
A tête-à-tête and lounges made by the M. & H. Schrenkeisen Manufacturing Company.

Center table with ormolu mounts and porcelain and metal plaques. Attributed to Pottier and Stymus. *Photograph courtesy of the Lyndhurst Corporation.*
$7000-10,000

Library tables [above] and marble top tables [left and below] made by the M. & H. Schrenkeisen Manufacturing Company.

Neo-Grec cabinet. *Photograph courtesy of the Art Institute of Chicago.* $3000-5000

Cabinet with marquetry, brass plaque and black marble top. Attributed to Herter Brothers. *Photograph courtesy of the Lyndhurst Corporation.* $8000-12,000

Cabinet by Alexander Roux. *Photograph courtesy of the Metropolitan Museum of Art.* $8000-12,000

Maple and bird's eye maple Faux bamboo armoire. Maker unknown. *Photograph courtesy of Sotheby's L.A.* $3000-5000

Hall stand made by the M. & H. Schrenkeisen Manufacturing Company.

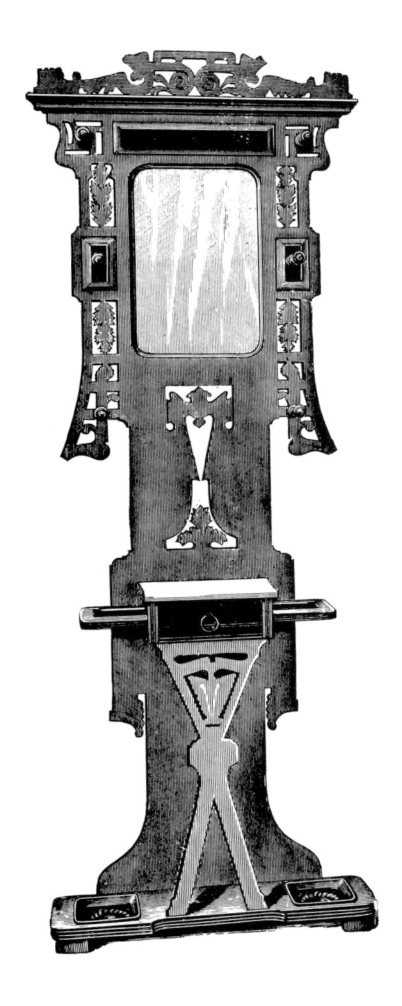

Three hall stands made by the M. & H. Schrenkeisen Manufacturing Company.

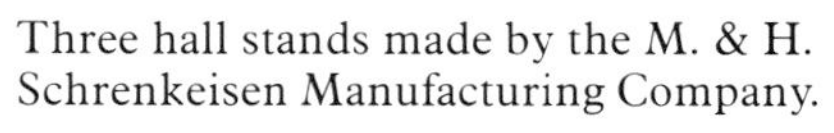

Carte de Visite by J.P. Weckman, Cincinnati, Ohio.

Carte de Visite by Sperber, late G.A. Uhle & Son, Allegheny, Pennsylvania.

Moorish Furniture

The Moorish furniture of 1876 to 1900 represents the triumph of the upholsterer over the cabinetmaker; the spell of the romantic novel like "Alhambre" by Washington Irving, and the mystery of the Orient as seen on the Grand Tour. It was a particular favorite for a Gentleman's smoking room. The style was probably introduced by Robert Conner in 1842 in his "Cabinet Makers Assistant" where he showed a Turkish sofa.

In 1848, P.T. Barnum built the Moorish mansion "Iranistan" in Connecticut. 1851 saw the construction of "Longwood" in Mississippi, an octagonal villa with Moorish cupola and porches.

1876 brought "Horticultural Hall" to the Philadelphia Centennial Exposition which had and Indian Portico of Iron.

In 1884, J.D. Rockefeller had a Moorish room created in his house at 53rd Street in New York City.

Room setting in the Lockwood Mathews Mansion.

Olana, 1870-1874, designed by Frederic Church in consultation with Calvert Vaux as a summer villa for the artist. *Photograph courtesy of New York State Office of Parks, Recreation and Historic Preservation, Bureau of Historic Sites, Olana State Historic Site, Taconic Region.*

One of a set of eight mahogany Moorish style side chairs at Olana, circa 1880. Brass casters are marked "20" "I.R. Comb Co.-Goodyear-1857". *Photograph courtesy of New York State Office of Parks, Recreation and Historic Preservation, Division for Historic Preservation, Bureau of Historic Sites, Olana State Historic Site, Taconic Region.* $1500-2500

Interior views of Olana, the summer home of F.E. Church, from photographs dating circa 1885. These rooms were designed by Church and reflect his masterly taste. He designed the rooms and the stencils, mixed the wall colors and placed the objects. *Photograph courtesy of New York State Office of Parks, Recreation and Historic Preservation, Division for Historic Preservation, Bureau of Historic Sites, Olana State Historic Site, Taconic Region.*

Left
Imogen, 1874, by Erastus Dow Palmer; bronze. Marked on back "E.D. PALMERS C/PARIS, 1874/F. BARREDINNE. FONDEUR". Church and Palmer were close friends and Palmer advised Church in the construction of his summer villa, Olana. The bust was a gift from Palmer. *Photograph courtesy of New York State Office of Parks, Recreation and Historic Preservation, Division for Historic Preservation, Bureau of Historic Sites, Olana State Historic Site, Taconic Region.*

Right
Wall shelf; designed and painted by Frederic Edwin Church to hold the bronze portrait bust "Imogen". The wooden shelf is painted deep blue with gilt linear design. *Photograph courtesy of New York State Office of Parks, Recreation and Historic Preservation, Division for Historic Preservation, Bureau of Historic Sites, Olana State Historic Site, Taconic Region.*

Below
Interior in the Moorish style. *Photograph courtesy of Yale University Library.*

Interior in the Moorish style. *Photograph courtesy of Yale University Library.*

Beds manufactured by the Ott Lounge Company and shown in their 1890 catalog.

Interior in the Moorish style. *Photograph courtesy of Yale University Library.*

Notes on...

Notes on Carpet of the Period

Ingrain: Kidderminster or Kilmarnoch, Scotch carpet. It has no pile and both sides are serviceable. These carpets were especially popular in the Empire period.
Wiltons: Produced in Wiltshire, England had a pile made of loops. The loops were then cut. These carpets were used for stairs as well as floors.
Brussels: Similar to Wilton except the loops of its pile are uncut.
Axminster: Most valuable of the period carpets. They were hand woven in one piece. In 1839 it occurred to Mr. Templeton, a paisley shawl manufacturer, that the process he used could be adapted and applied to Axminster carpets. This reduced the price, although they remained costly. In 1882 the firm of Templeton & Company of Glasgow hand-wove an Axminster carpet for the library of the White House. The designs imitated Turkey Carpet.
"Patent Axminster": Was shown at the 1851 London Exhibition by Templeton and Company. It closely resembled the costly original Axminster, but was entirely woven rather than composed of separate tufts tied by hand.

Notes on Cenus and Immigration

The 1840 Census shows a total population in the United States of 8, 688,532. According to the breakdown, 18,003 men were engaged in furniture making.

The 1850 Census shows 83,580 men engaged in furniture making; 37,359 as cabinetmakers, 1,742 as carvers and gilders, 112 frame makers, 2,592 upholsterers and the balance in allied trades. The total population was 11,837,660.

The 1860 Census shows a total population of 16,085,204. The value in 1869 of house furnishings (finished commodities) for domestic consumption was 40 million.

The 1870 Census shows a total population of 19,493,565. The value of house furnishings in 1879 was 56 million.

Notes on Expositions

In 1847, Prince Albert (Queen Victoria's consort) sponsored a Society of Arts Exhibition in London. It was a great success and the Prince's friend, designer Henry Cole, encouraged him to stage the first International Exposition. This Universal Exposition was held in the Crystal Palace in London in 1851. It was the first exposition to give the decorative arts a major roll. Henry Cole was one of the organizers of the Exposition. The Crystal Palace was built in 1851 and enclosed nineteen acres of London's Hyde Park. It was built of iron and glass and housed 15,000 exhibitors. When it closed it was moved to

Sydenham where it remained until 1936 when it burned down. Some of the American firms that exhibited were: Cornelius, Nunn and Clark, Doe Hazzelton, and the American Chair Company.

The London event inspired the Crystal Palace Exhibition in New York in 1853. It was designed by Joseph Paxton. Alexander Roux, Ringuet Le Prince, Marcotte and Dessoir exhibited at it.

Exhibitions became so popular that there was one in Paris in 1855, London in 1862, Paris in 1867, London in 1871, Vienna in 1873, then the largest and most exciting of all, the Centennial Exhibition in Philadelphia in 1876.

More exhibitions after this were held in Paris in 1878, Sydney in 1879, Chicago in 1893, and the 1889 Paris exhibition for which the Eiffel Tower was erected.

Famous men who once were in the Furniture Trade

William M. Tweed (Boss Tweed) was born April 3, 1823. His father, Richard, had been an apprentice to Thomas Ash. The Windsor chair maker, until setting up his own business at 24 Cherry Street. William worked in his father's shop as a youth, then he went away to school. In 1844 he opened his own chair shop at 325 Pearl Street, New York. He kept the shop open for three years and then turned to organizing volunteer fire companies. In 1858 he went into politics.

Hiram Powers, who later became a well known sculptor worked as a chair maker in Cincinnati in 1834 for Plum & Water. He also did mechanical work for the clock maker Luman Watson.

Samuel Lee the landscape painter worked as a chair decorator in Cincinnati from 1823-1831.

Andrew Harkness, the industrialist, began his business in 1819 as a turner in Cincinnati.

Notes on Fabrics of the Period

Brocatelle: Typical examples have patterns in slight relief on a satin ground or the raised design may be satin. It is similar to Lampas. The effect is obtained by the use of an extra weft or wefts, one of which is linen. The linen weft does not show on the surface.
Lampas: A fancy compound satin. A fabric of satin weave with one or more extra warps or wefts or both, that are used to make a pattern. Looks like a two color damask but is not reversible since its back is plain mat.
Damask: Reversible solid color fabric with a woven design that appears mat on a glossy ground on the face, and glossy on a mat ground on the back of the fabric.
Satin: Silk fabric with a smooth glossy surface and a mat back.
Velvet: Fabric with a close standing pile on the face (the right side). Velvets are woven with one or more extra warps. These supplementary ways threads pass over metal rods that pull them up into loops. A knife can then be run along a groove in the rod, cutting each loop open into two tufts. This is solid cut velvet. If the rods are withdrawn, leaving the standing loops, you have uncut velvet or velour. In cisele velvet, some of the loops are cut, and some left uncut, to carry out a design.

Warp: Lengthwise threads that run from one end of the cloth to the other end.
Weft: Run crosswise from selvege to selvege (edge to edge) intersecting the warp threads.
Gimp: Replaced nail heads for the finished look around upholstered pieces about 1830.

Floor Coverings other than Carpet

In 1822 a carpeting substitute was invented in Philadelphia. It was made of highly varnished paper that was painted in a number of patterns. When finished it had the appearance of oil cloth floor covers. It was said to last five years, and was considerably cheaper than oil cloth.

In 1870 parquet floor or "wooden carpet" gained in popularity. Halbut of Brooklyn made a parquet floor one-fourth inch thick. The pieces of parquet were shipped, prepared in place and glued to a cloth. A local carpenter then shaped the floor to the room. *The Decorator and Furnisher* for October 1890 stated: "The combination of oriental rug and a floor of wood is very artistic".

Notes on Lighting of the Period

Argand lamps used sperm oil or lard oil. They went through several transformations and by 1840 were known as Sinumbra lamps. The Sinumbra lamp was preferred over the Argand because it projected no shadow. The Sinumbra

Steam ship interior, circa 1880. *Photograph courtesy Louisiana State University Library.*

Interior view of unidentified home, circa 1885. *Photograph courtesy Louisiana State University Library.*

may be used synonymously with the term Annula and astral lamp. Gas first appeared when a Baltimore company was organized in 1816. By the year 1821 they had 73 customers and the city of Baltimore used gas as lighting. Another early gas company was chartered in Philadelphia in 1835 and by the following year had 670 customers. Gas was very late coming to rural areas (if at all) and Sinumbra/Astra lamps were used by country homes until 1854 when kerosene was developed, and some switched over to kerosene lamps.

In the Sunumbra/Astral lamp, the reservoir is round and located within the shade. These lamps were designed to burn whole oil.

The Solar lamp was designed to burn cheaper oils or lard. Solar lamps are distinguished by the location of the reservoir beneath the burner.

By 1845 Christian Cornelius was the largest manufacturer of lamps in the United States. Other prominent makers were Baldwin Gardiner of New York, William Shaw of Boston, and Clark Coit and Cargill of New York.

The Newell lamp was patented on October 4, 1853 (#10,099) by John Newell of Boston. It was the new and improved lamp for burning camphene without danger of explosion. The reservoir incorporated two perforated metal cylinders, one inside the other. This lamp was the subject of heated controversy in the pages of scientific America.

Notes on Transportation and its effect on Furniture manufacture

The year 1811 marked the first successful steamboat journey from Pittsburgh to New Orleans. By 1817 there were seventeen steamboats in regular use, and by 1855 the number swelled to 727. These boats provided service not only on the Mississippi and Ohio Rivers, but its tributaries. By 1860 the steam boat covered 2,280 miles up the Missouri River to Fort Benson, Montana. This allowed raw material to be shipped out of the west and finished goods to be brought in. Steamboats transported much of the bulky freight until the 1850s when railroads began to make heavy inroads. These goods were needed to serve a population in the Mississippi and Ohio Valleys that had grown from one million in 1810, to two million in 1820 and exceeded six million by 1840.

The increased population and the means to transport the goods was a factor in relocation of the furniture industry to the Midwest by the 1860s and 70s. There was also the factors of proximity to raw materials and the waves of immigrants moving into the Midwest.

Notes on Veneering and Laminating

Veneering is the process of overlaying a prepared surface or ground with thin wood. This art was known to the ancients. Pliny spoke of it as a recent invention in his time, and discussed it in terms of converting the cheaper into the most valued woods. Veneering is done primarily for esthetic purposes. In 16th century Italy, marquetry and intarsia panels often had their face veneer pictures laid on a cross banding, glued in turn to a solid band.

Laminating is an extension of veneering in the sense that many layers of wood are overlaid, providing a strong lightweight material. Laminating is done for structural purposes. It not only adds strength and stability but enables one to obtain larger dimensions, free from natural defects, more so than nature provides. Timber shrinks across the grain (in width). Timber is stronger in length then it is across the grain. Therefore, the most practical way to make large sheets of stable wood and equal strength in both directions is to glue and press veneers in layers arranged at right angles to each other, until the desired thickness is obtained.

In order to veneer one must first have a caul. Cauls are a means of conveying heat and transmitting pressure to the whole surface of a veneer at once. In cauling veneers, the veneer is held in place over the ground until the parts cool and consolidate. Cauls must be perfectly parallel to the ground and must be uniform and distributed over the entire extent.

Cauls were made in 1853 of pine wood and sometimes of wood with canvas continuations for abrupt curves. Cauls were also made of large bags partially filled with hot sand. These were used for veneering hollow and/or irregularly shaped surfaces. Canvas or girth web was used in cauling cylindrical grounds such as pillars or pedestals. The pressure on cauls was usually by screw action.

Mr. John London patented an apparatus by which the same veneer could be carried continuously without a break or joint over all forms of curved surfaces or angles. This was affected by a series of cauls hinged together and acted upon by direct screw pressure, and by lever power supported by ratch work. See: *Repository of Inventions*, 1850 Vol. XV. Examples of the efficiency of this apparatus were displayed at the Great London Exhibition of 1851.

Making veneer layers for laminating

Making the veneer layers for laminating from pages 133-41 of the *Architect Review Supplement* September, 1939.

1. Logs are cut to length desired, peeled of bark and soaked in water.
2. Logs are put on veneer lathes to remove the rough outer wood; then the veneer is peeled off in a continuous ribbon.
3. The sheets are trimmed to size and passed on rollers through drying machines.
4. The core sheets are trimmed to size and passed on rollers through drying machines. The core sheet is covered with adhesive as it is passed between rollers and dipped in glue.
5. The sheets are pressed together in a hydraulic press.
6. Sheets are left to dry, then scrapped and trimmed.

Bibliography

ARCHIVES

The Historic New Orleans Collection.

BOOKS

Bjerkoe, Ethel. *The Cabinetmakers of America*. Doubleday, 1957. Revised edition: Exton, Pennsylvania; Schiffer Publishing Ltd., 1978.
Butler, Joseph T. *American Antiques, 1800-1900*. Odyssey Press, 1965.
Candee, Hellen C. *Decorative Styles in the House*. 1861.
Centuries and Styles of the American Chair. New York: E.P. Dutton, 1972.
The City Built on Wood. Ann Arbor: Edwards Brothers, 1955.
Clifford, Chandler R. *The Decorative Periods.*
Comstock, Helen. *American Furniture, 17th, 18th, & 19th Century Styles*. New York: Viking Press, 1962. Exton: Schiffer Publishing Ltd., 1980.
Fairbanks, J. and Bates, E. *American Furniture 1620 to the Present*. New York: R. Marek Publishing, 1979.
Fitzgerald. *3 Centuries of American Furniture*. Englewood Cliffs, New Jersey: Prentice Hall, 1981.
The Glorious Enterprise. New York: Watkins Glen, 1973.
A Guide to Victorian Antiques. New York: Harper Brothers, 1949.
Hanks, D. *Innovative Furniture in America*. New York: Horizon Press, 1981.
A History of the Furniture Industry in Grand Rapids. Ann Arbor: Edwards Brothers, 1955.
The Manufacturers of Cincinnati. Robert D. Clark & Company, 1978.
McClinton, K. *Collecting American Victorian Antiques.* New York: Scribner Sons, 1966.
Modern Dwellings. Holly, 1878.
Nesbit, Wilbur. *The Story of Berkey & Gay.*
19th Century America. New York: Metropolitan Museum of Art, 1970.
Oliver, J.L. *The Development and Structure of the Furniture Industry.* Pergamon Press, 1966.
Ormsbe, T. *Field Guide to American Furniture.* Boston: Little, Brown & Company, 1952.
Otto, C. *American Furniture of the 19th Century.* New York: Viking Press, 1965.
Philadelphia Museum of Art. *Authentic Furniture of the Great Philadelphia Cabinetmakers.* 1935.
Philadelphia Museum of Art. "Bulletin" XLVIII No. 237. 1953.
Philadelphia Museum of Art. *Georgian Decorative Arts.* J. Downs, 1931.
Schwarts, M. and Stanek, E. and True, D. *The Furniture of John H. Belter and*

The Rococo Revival. New York: Dutton, 1981.
Seale, William. *The Tasteful Intulude.* Praeger Publishing, 1975.
Silman, Benjamin and Goodrich, Charles. *The World of Sci, Art & Industry.*
Styes, Boger. *Complete Guide to Furniture.* New York: Scribner, 1959.
Tracy, B., Johnson, M., Schwartz, M., and Boorsch, S. *19th Century America: Furniture and other Decorative Arts.* New York: Metropolitan Museum of Art, 1973.
Weise, A.J. *History of Troy and Vicinity.*
Winterthur Portfolio No. 9. Ken Ames, University Press of Virginia, 1974.
Winterthur Portfolio No. 13 - American Furniture and its Makers. University Press of Virginia.
The Year of the Century 1876. New York: Scribners & Sons, 1966.

MAGAZINES

Art and Antiques, 1980-82.
Art Amateur, 1886-87.
American Collector, 1936.
Antiques Magazine, 1940-80.
The Decorator & Furniture, 1981.
Harpers Weekly.
The Michigan Artisan, 1880-1890.
19th Century Magazine, all issues.

NEWSPAPERS

The New Orleans Piciune Times, 1840-1870.

THESIS

Streifthan, Donna. *Cincinnatti Cabinet and Chair Makers, 1819-1930.* Ph D thesis. Ohio State University, 1970.
Vincent, Clair. M.A. thesis. Institute of Fine Arts, New York University, 1963.

Index

E

F

G

H

I

J

K

L

W